The Birds of Tikal

NUMBER TWELVE:
THE W. L. MOODY, JR., NATURAL HISTORY SERIES

Temple II in the Main Plaza. (Photograph by J. L. Tveten)

Randell A. Beavers

The Birds of Tikal

An Annotated Checklist for Tikal National Park
and Petén, Guatemala

Texas A&M University Press
College Station

ON COVER: OCELLATED TURKEY *(Agriocharis ocellata)*
Nowhere else but Tikal is the Ocellated Turkey so abundant and note-worthy. Apparently, this was the case even over 130 years ago, as indicated by the comments of Lutley Sclater and Osbert Salvin on this turkey in an 1859 issue of *Ibis:* "From all accounts, the little-known district, of which the Lake of Petén forms the chief feature, is its headquarters; and there it would appear to be of not unfrequent occurrence." Color painting by John P. O'Neill.

The paper used in this book meets the minimum requirements
of the American National Standard for Permanence of Paper
for Printed Library Materials, Z39.48-1984.
Binding materials have been chosen for durability. ∞

Library of Congress Cataloging-in-Publication Data

Beavers, Randell A., 1950–
        The birds of Tikal : an annotated checklist for Tikal National
Park and Petén, Guatemala / Randell A. Beavers. — 1st ed.
            p.   cm. — (W.L. Moody, Jr., natural history series ; no. 12)
        Includes index.
        ISBN 0-89096-525-0 (cloth); 0-89096-518-8 (paper)
        1. Birds–Guatemala–Parque Nacional Tikal.   2. Birds–
Guatemala–Petén (Dept.)   I. Title.   II. Series.
QL687.G9B43   1992
598.2972812–dc20   92-2919
                                                                CIP

Contents

Figures

Acknowledgments

This checklist could not have been completed without the assistance and cooperation of many individuals. I wish to thank all of those who so generously shared their personal bird records with me. They include Peter C. Alden, Robert A. Askins, Bob H. Barth, Robert A. Behrstock, Chris Benesh, Marcia L. Braun, Ron W. Braun, Howard P. Brokaw, Elbert C. Cleaveland, Dale J. Delaney, Richard A. Erickson, Emery M. Froelich, Steve N. G. Howell, J. Peter Jenny and staff members of the Peregrine Fund, Lawrence Kilham, Katrina T. Ladwig, Christopher W. Leahy, Jane A. Lyons, G. Frank Oatman, Lina J. Prairie, Noble S. Proctor, Rose Ann Rowlett, Jan P. Smith, Judith Sparrow, Dave Stejskal, Russell K. Thorstrom, and Jay P. Vannini. I am particularly grateful to Dale J. Delaney, J. Peter Jenny, Christopher W. Leahy, and G. Frank Oatman for their valuable contributions and detailed attention given to this project. Their many years of experience in the area added greatly to the scope of this work. Raymond A. Paynter, Jr., of the Harvard University Museum of Comparative Zoology is appreciated for the data provided from Frank B. Smithe's collection and for sharing his special knowledge of the ornithology of this region. Nathan Kraucunas of the Milwaukee Public Museum and Graham S. Cowles of the British Museum (Natural History) were helpful in providing historical specimen data from Petén. Thanks are also extended to Carl H. Aiken, John B. Baird, Robbie A. Beavers, Carol N. Bookout, Marcia L. Braun, Ron W. Braun, Bill V. Mealy, Jim S. Powell, Pat P. Powell, Linda R. Schooley, Jeffrey G. Schultz, Gloria A. Tveten, and John L. Tveten for their assistance in the field.

I am deeply grateful to Guatemala's tourism department, INGUAT, for their assistance during my stays in Guatemala, and to the Spring Branch Independent School District Board of Trustees for allowing me to be away from my position at the Science Center to conduct the fieldwork. I appreciate the special efforts made by Karen Govorchin of PCI Tours, Inc. for expediting much of my travel arrangements to Guatemala. Antonio Ortiz, proprietor of the Jungle Lodge, is thanked for his never-ending hospitality.

I appreciate the thorough review of the manuscript by Steve N. G. Howell, G. Frank Oatman, John P. O'Neill, Raymond A. Paynter, Jr., and John L. Tveten. Their comments and suggestions were most helpful. My wife, Robbie A. Beavers, spent endless hours preparing the manuscript. Through her, I have come to know the true meaning of patience.

John P. O'Neill (front color cover), John L. Tveten (most black-and-white photographs), and Donna L. Warren (maps) are commended for their artistry and skills, which have created a more attractive and useful checklist.

Special thanks goes to my friend and colleague Carl H. Aiken for his encouragement throughout the project and for introducing me to the world of tropical ornithology. To him, this work is dedicated.

The Birds of Tikal

Introduction

Tikal National Park was established in 1956, the first national park in all of Middle America. Located in the north-central part of the Department of Petén, Guatemala, Tikal is approximately 576 square kilometers (222 square miles) in area and is best known for its extensive Mayan ruins. The park is also part of a much larger multinational Biosphere Reserve system that will eventually encompass adjoining biospheres in Mexico and Belize totaling 5 million acres. The central Petén region is dominated by low rolling hills of porous Oligocene limestone, accounting for the limited amount of permanent surface water (e.g., Lagos Petén-Itzá and Yaxhá). Even during the rainy season, from May through November, only a few surface streams exist. The dry season runs from December through April, the period most tourists visit Tikal. Annual rainfall varies from year to year, ranging from 1,000 to 2,400 millimeters (40 to 95 inches). All but approximately 300 millimeters of this rainfall occurs during the rainy season, reaching monthly peaks of 250 to 300 millimeters (10 to 12 inches). Temperatures vary as well, from evening lows of 15° to 22° C (59° to 72° F) to daytime highs of 28° to 35° C (82° to 95° F) (Smithe 1966).

According to Holdridge (1967), central Petén lies in a transitional area between the tropical dry and tropical moist semi-

4

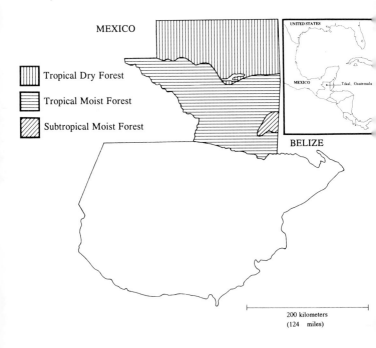

MEXICO

Tropical Dry Forest

Tropical Moist Forest

Subtropical Moist Forest

BELIZE

UNITED STATES

MEXICO   Tikal, Guatemala

200 kilometers
(124   miles)

Map 1. Holdridge Life Zones of Petén

deciduous forests (map 1). To the north, on the Yucatán Peninsula, the forest gradually yields to a scrub forest as the climate becomes drier. To the south, in the Caribbean lowland, the rainfall increases and the forest becomes more evergreen, stratified, and diverse. Perhaps more appropriately, Lundell (1937) refers to the central Petén forest as a quasi-rainforest, suggesting the presence of the basic floral, faunal, structural, and rainfall characteristics of a typical rainforest, but to a lesser degree than found in more equatorial rainforests.

Unfortunately, slash-and-burn and clear-cutting practices outside the park have drastically reduced the more productive primary forest to a mosaic pattern of forest fragments (Burnham, Jenny, and Turley 1989). It is not surprising that a majority of the species appearing to show recent increases in their relative abundances are those which typically prefer clearings, second-growth forests, and other disturbed habitats (e.g., Cattle Egret, Black Vulture, and Great-tailed Grackle). Conversely, several primary forest-dependent species seem to be experiencing dramatic declines in their relative abundances (e.g., Orange-breasted Falcon and Spotted Wood-Quail). Nevertheless, a significant amount of protected and undisturbed tropical forest still exists in Tikal, supporting a diverse population of birdlife.

Even though the majority of Tikal's eighty thousand annual tourists visit the park to see the magnificent ruins, an increasing number trek to the area to watch birds and other wildlife. This book is designed especially for these bird enthusiasts. This checklist is not an identification guide, but rather a detailed account of the bird species found in the region, providing information on when, where, and in what numbers each species should be expected. Several field guides are available to aid in the identification of the region's birds. *A Field Guide to Mexican Birds,* by Roger Tory Peterson and Edward L. Chalif, is among the most widely used and is now offered in an expanded Spanish version (see Selected References).

A Note on Bird Identification in the Tropics

Birding in the tropics can be very rewarding, but it can also be somewhat frustrating to the beginner, as a greater number of species are difficult to find and identify in the tropics than in the temperate regions (i.e., many species are secretive and similar in appearance). However, tropical species generally occupy narrower niches in their environment and tend to exhibit more specific feeding, nesting, and habitat requirements and behaviors than their temperate counterparts. Even though these specific requirements and behaviors are not as clearly delineated in Petén species as with those found in more southern tropics, there is enough specialization among many species to warrant their use as "field clues" that can aid in location and identification. This is the purpose of including habitat preferences and certain behavioral characteristics in the checklist. If used in conjunction with physical and vocal characteristics of birds noted in field guides, this checklist should provide the added information to enhance one's success in the field.

Traveling and Staying in Central Petén

Most visitors reach the Tikal area by one of two routes: flying in from Guatemala City to Flores (the airport is actually in Santa Elena) or driving in from Belize. The latter route is advised only during the dry season, as the road usually becomes impassable once the rains begin in May. To drive in from Belize, vehicles may be rented or daily buses taken from Melchor de Mencos, Guatemala, or from San Ignacio, Belize. Allow at least a half-day for travel to the park using this route. It is also possible to drive (or ride the bus) in from the Department of Izabal to the south. This route should be attempted only by the seasoned traveler and is not recommended by the author.

Daily flights are available from Guatemala City on Aerovías, Aero Quetzal, Aviateca, Aviones Comerciales de Guatemala, and Tapsa. Since good birding opportunities begin immediately along the road to the park, it is recommended to hire a taxi van, rather than taking a commuter bus or one of the transports provided by the lodges. The benefit of being able to stop and bird at your own pace is well worth the extra expense of hiring a taxi. At Tikal, taxi vans are always available for transfers back to Santa Elena, or for half-day and full-day excursions outside the park.

There are numerous hotels in the Flores–Santa Elena area and a new Camino Real near Lago Petén-Itzá, but to take full advantage of the birding opportunities in Tikal, it is best to stay at one of the lodges in the park. The Jungle Lodge, Jaguar Inn, and Hotel Tikal Inn offer simple but comfortable accommodations at modest prices. For reservations and current rates at the lodges, contact the Jungle Lodge, 29 Calle 18-01, Zona 12, Guatemala City, Guatemala CA, or telephone from the United States 011-502-2-760294; the Jaguar Inn, Tikal National Park, Petén, Guatemala, CA, telephone 011-502-9-500002; Hotel Tikal Inn, Tikal National Park,

Flores, Petén, Guatemala, CA. Reservations should be made
well in advance.

Ornithological History of Petén

The inaccessible nature of Petén has undoubtedly played a
role in the sporadic and limited study of birds in the region.
Ornithological exploration did not begin until the mid-nine-
teenth century, when a small number of ornithologists and
amateurs took a few specimens in passing through the area.
Records indicate the earliest collections were made in 1847 by
a French traveler named M. Morelet (Sclater and Salvin 1859;
Salvin and Godman 1879–1904; Griscom 1932). Unfortunately, a complete list of the birds collected on this trip was
never published. In 1856 Joseph Leyland visited Lake Petén-
Itzá and collected a small number of specimens (Moore 1859;
Sclater and Salvin 1859). Osbert Salvin passed through the
Lake Petén-Itzá area in 1861 on his long journey by foot from
Alta Verapaz to Belize (Salvin 1866; Salvin and Godman
1879–1904). In early 1887 Colonel N. S. Goss, a Kansas orni-
thologist, made a short side trip to Yaxhá from Belize, collect-
ing two Ocellated Turkeys (Lantz 1899).

The birdlife of Petén did not receive full attention until
1931, when Josselyn Van Tyne visited Uaxactún as part of a
University of Michigan expedition. In addition to his own
thorough findings, Van Tyne (1935) reported on the 167 species collected by Harry Malleis in 1923, and on the small collections of P. W. Shufeldt in 1917 and E. G. Holt in 1926.
Shufeldt again collected in the Laguna Perdida area, northwest of Lake Petén-Itzá, in 1920 (Land 1970). An Italian natu-
ralist, Alulah M. Taibel, visited the Flores area from May to

September 1932 and reported 87 species (Taibel 1955). The list of Petén birds was nearing a total of 240 species at the end of this period.

It was nearly twenty-five years before bird study resumed in Petén, with Frank B. Smithe's (with others) Tikal project between 1956 and 1962 (Smithe and Paynter 1963). This is the most extensive ornithological study thus far conducted in Petén and resulted in the popular field guide *The Birds of Tikal* (Smithe 1966). This guide provides an excellent account of each species reported in the park through the early 1960s and remains quite useful today. A *Milwaukee Journal*/Milwaukee Public Museum expedition along the Salinas, Usumacinta, and Pasión rivers in southwestern Petén was led by William Schultz between February and March of 1962. The unpublished specimen records of the museum indicate 46 species were collected from Petén on this expedition. With additional Petén records noted by Land (1970), the total list of birds reported from this department stood at 372 species.

Over the next twenty-five years the only publications reporting on the distribution and occurrence of birds from the Petén include Brodkin and Brodkin (1981), Ellis and Whaley (1981), and Wendelken and Martin (1986). Together, these reports added eight species to the list of Petén birds.

Most of Petén's recent bird records are in the form of unpublished observation notes compiled by many reliable field observers and a series of progress reports of the Peregrine Fund's ongoing raptor censusing project in Tikal (Burnham, Jenny, and Turley 1988, 1989, 1990). Particularly useful to the development of this checklist were those records compiled by Peter Alden (reporting his data from 1967–71), Robert

Askins (reporting his data from 1970–71 and 1977–78), Robert A. Behrstock (reporting his data from 1975 and 1991–92), Elbert C. Cleaveland (reporting his data and that of Russell K. Thorstrom from 1988–89), Dale J. Delaney (reporting his data and that of co-observer Steven Hilty from 1988–90), Steve N. G. Howell (reporting his data and that of Sophie Webb from 1984–92), J. Peter Jenny (reporting his data from 1986–90), Christopher W. Leahy (reporting his data and that of Major Bowes, Tom Davis, Michael Gochfeld, Lawrence Kilham, Noble Proctor, and Robert Ridgely from 1967–79), Jane Lyons (reporting her data and that of co-observers Bob Barth and Bill Fritz from 1989–90), G. Frank Oatman (reporting his data and that of co-observers John Arvin, Dave Stejskal, and Bret Whitney from 1969–91), Rose Ann Rowlett (reporting her data from 1975–81), and Jan Smith (reporting his data from 1977). These reports, along with the author's data collected between 1986 and 1992, resulted in many significant records for the region (see Beavers et al. 1991). At least 404 species of birds have now been reported from this department; future studies will no doubt add to this number.

The Checklist Area and Its Habitats
The checklist area incorporates all of Petén, with emphasis on the central portions of the department that are most frequently visited by birders. These central portions include the Flores–Santa Elena and Lago Petén-Itzá areas and the adjoining roads and roadsides southwest approximately 35 kilometers (22 miles) to the La Libertad area, south approximately 50 kilometers (31 miles) along the road to the Santo Toribio area, east approximately 50 kilometers (31 miles) along the Belize road

to the Nakum-Yaxhá-Naranjo area, and north to the main park entrance; all of Tikal National Park; and the road north approximately 19 kilometers (12 miles) to the ruins of Uaxactún. The more remote regions of western, northern, and southern Petén are also included in the area covered by this checklist (e.g., areas west of Lago Petén-Itzá, north and west of Tikal, southeast to the San Luis–Poptún area, and southwest to the Rio de la Pasión) (Map 2).

To see as many species of birds as possible in (central) Petén, time must be spent both inside and outside Tikal National Park. The entire stretch of the main road from the Santa Elena airport to the park and a short distance down various side roads will produce many species unlikely to be found in the park itself. The main road to Tikal passes through a variety of habitats, including vast open areas with scattered trees (good for raptors), roadside second-growth forests, and abandoned milpas (Figure 1). The area along the roads to Poptún and Melchor de Mencos is somewhat hilly and dominated by clearings and abandoned milpas with thickets at lower elevations, and second-growth forests and fragmented primary forests on the hilltops (Figure 2). Farther south along the road to Poptún, the hills give way to a flatter savanna. Also, pine ridge habitat is found in extreme southeastern Petén, east of San Luis. Species more characteristic of the Caribbean lowlands have been reported from this region, including Nightingale Wren, Scarlet-rumped Tanager, and Rusty Sparrow. The road south to La Libertad passes through open grassland savanna with intermittent hills and scattered trees. On these roads outside of the park, look for such localized species as Little Tinamou, Gray-headed Kite, Zone-tailed Hawk, Pale-

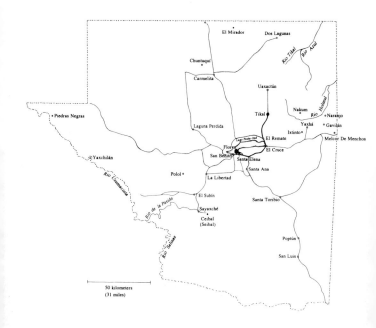

Map 2. The Department of El Petén

13

Figure 1. An abandoned milpa along the side of the road near Caoba provides foraging habitat for Ground-Doves and Grassquits. (Photograph by R. A. Beavers)

Figure 2. Mature second-growth forest on hilltops with cleared low areas along the road to Poptún. The first three kilometers of this road south of Santa Elena are quite productive and should be birded thoroughly. (Photograph by R. A. Beavers)

Figure 3. Lago Petén-Itzá provides an important habitat for many aquatic species. The eastern and western reaches of the lake seem to be the most productive areas for birding. (Photograph by J. L. Tveten)

vented Pigeon, Red-billed Pigeon, White-tipped Dove, Plain-breasted Ground-Dove, Striped Cuckoo, Ferruginous Pygmy-Owl, Rufous-breasted Spinetail, Great Antshrike, Cinnamon Becard, Black Catbird, Rufous-browed Peppershrike, Banana-quit, Crimson-collared Tanager, Grayish Saltator, Buff-throated Saltator, Olive Sparrow, Yellow-faced Grassquit, and Yellow-tailed Oriole. These species are annotated with the habitat code 4 (open or rather open areas) in the checklist, often in conjunction with the code L (localized), since many species have a localized distribution in Petén. East along the road to Melchor de Mencos, near the Yaxhá-Nakum-Naranjo area, look for the Band-backed Wren along remnant riparian woodlands, and for the Boat-billed Heron, Common Potoo, and Amazon Kingfisher along the streams created during the rainy season.

A limited number of aquatic areas provide an important habitat for several species of waterbirds that are otherwise un-common in central Petén. Lake Petén-Itzá is the largest body of water in Petén, roughly 3–5 kilometers (2–3 miles) wide and 25 kilometers (16 miles) long (Figure 3). During the win-ter and migration periods, look for Pied-billed Grebe, Brown Pelican, and various herons, egrets, gulls, terns, gallinules, and shorebirds. The most productive areas of the lake seem to be the west side near San Benito, the east side near El Remate, and along the north shore road near the Cerro Cahui Pre-serve. Aguadas (ponds) are scattered throughout the central Petén and can be found both inside and outside the park (Figure 4). Roadside aguadas (such as the one found at Paxca-mán) and aguadas Tikal, Dimmick, and San Antonio inside the park occasionally harbor Least Grebe, Bare-throated

Tiger-Heron, Ruddy Crake, Gray-necked Wood-Rail, Sungrebe, Limpkin, Northern Jacana, and several species of kingfishers. Snail Kite can sometimes be found on the larger aguadas, as well as in the more secluded areas of Lake Petén-Itzá. Aquatic habitats are more prevalent in southwestern Petén (e.g., Rio de la Pasión and associated tributaries), and as one might expect, the avifauna varies somewhat from that found in the remainder of the department. Such notable species as the Black-bellied Whistling-Duck, Great Potoo, and Chestnut-headed Oropendola have been reported from this region and are probably resident there. More extensive bird study is still needed here and in the wetlands of extreme western Petén.

The central portions of Tikal offer days of excellent birding within walking distance of the lodging area (Map 3). More than 100 species of birds can easily be seen here each day, except perhaps during the summer period. The open areas around the lodges and villages and along the airstrip should be explored thoroughly (Figure 5). Plain Chachalaca, Ocellated Turkey, Red-lored Parrot, Keel-billed Toucan, Golden-fronted Woodpecker, Social Flycatcher, Brown Jay, Spot-breasted Wren, Lesser Greenlet, Yellow-throated Euphonia, White-collared Seedeater, Melodious Blackbird, and Montezuma Oropendola are some of the species to be seen daily around the lodges. Along the 1½-mile airstrip, watch overhead for various raptors, pigeons, swifts, and martins. The forest edge and thickets along the sides of the airstrip can also be very productive for woodland species.

The trails to the major ruin sites are well maintained and offer relatively easy access through the tall tropical forest.

18

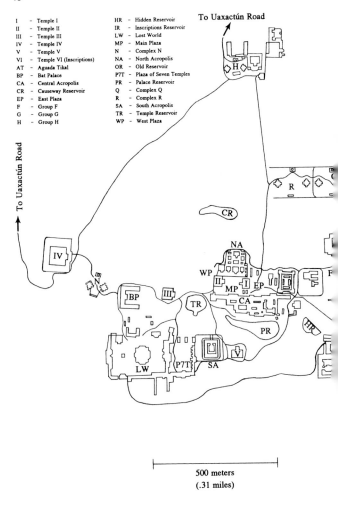

I	–	Temple I	HR	–	Hidden Reservoir
II	–	Temple II	IR	–	Inscriptions Reservoir
III	–	Temple III	LW	–	Lost World
IV	–	Temple IV	MP	–	Main Plaza
V	–	Temple V	N	–	Complex N
VI	–	Temple VI (Inscriptions)	NA	–	North Acropolis
AT	–	Aguada Tikal	OR	–	Old Reservoir
BP	–	Bat Palace	P7T	–	Plaza of Seven Temples
CA	–	Central Acropolis	PR	–	Palace Reservoir
CR	–	Causeway Reservoir	Q	–	Complex Q
EP	–	East Plaza	R	–	Complex R
F	–	Group F	SA	–	South Acropolis
G	–	Group G	TR	–	Temple Reservoir
H	–	Group H	WP	–	West Plaza

Map 3. Trails and Roads of Central Areas, Tikal National Park (Locations

of trails and structures are only approximations and are not to scale.)

Figure 4. Dense aquatic vegetation supports a diverse bird community at Aguada Tikal near the lodges. This aguada should be checked daily for wading and gallinaceous birds. (Photograph by J. L. Tveten)

Figure 5. Bungalows at the Jungle Lodge. The easily accessible areas around the lodges offer excellent leisure birding. Over forty species of birds have been seen (or heard) from this courtyard in the first hour of light. (Photograph by J. L. Tveten)

This tall forest is dominated by zapote (*Manilkara*), mahogany (*Swietenia*), ramón (*Brosimum*), Spanish cedar (*Cedrela*), amapola (*Bernoullia*), and kapok (*Ceiba*) and is found in the higher elevations of the better-drained central park region. The canopy here can reach a height of 45 meters (150 feet), often promoting a dark and rather open understory (Figure 6). Where the tall forest is not overly mature and more sunlight penetrates the canopy, the understory can be much denser. This dense tall forest is often peripherally associated with the open tall forest at slightly lower elevations. Most of the forest-dependent species will, of course, be found in the tall forests of Tikal and are annotated with the habitat codes 1 and 2 (open and dense tall forests) in the checklist. While walking the trails and roads to the ruins, look and listen particularly for flocks attending army ant swarms and for mixed-species flocks that occasionally move through the forest. In these flocks, watch for Plain Xenops, Ruddy Woodcreeper, Olivaceous Woodcreeper, Barred Woodcreeper, Dot-winged Antwren, Tawny-crowned Greenlet, Olive-backed Euphonia, Gray-headed Tanager, Black-throated Shrike-Tanager, and Red-throated Ant-Tanager. The forest edge, adjacent to most ruins and along major trails and roads, should be explored regularly (Figure 7). This transitional zone is quite productive, providing opportunities for open area, forest, and forest border species (habitat code 3 in checklist). Also, birders can gain access above the tall forest canopy by climbing the larger temples. Temple IV, the tallest Mayan structure, is one of the most productive ruins from which to observe raptors and upper-canopy species (Figure 8).

A smaller part of Tikal is occupied by the low forest. This

forest occurs in the lower, poorly drained areas called *bajos,*
where the canopy rarely exceeds 15 meters (50 feet). There are
two types of low forests found in central Petén: the escobal
palm forest and the unique tintal forest. The escobal forest is
dominated by the palms *Cryosophila argentea,* the *palma de
escoba* ("broom palm"), and *Sabal morrisiana,* highly prized as
roof thatch. Good stands of the escobal forest can be found approximately 3½ kilometers (2.2 miles) north from the central
regions of the park along the road to Uaxactún and along the
trail to Yaxhá, 1–1½ kilometers (1 mile) past the end of the
Tikal airstrip (Figure 9). Low thickets are common throughout the escobal forest, where Slaty-breasted Tinamou, Ruddy
Quail-Dove, Tody Motmot, and Buff-throated Foliage-gleaner
can be found.

The tintal forest was named from the Spanish word *tinto,*
meaning "dyed" or "stained," and refers to the dominance of
the logwood tree, *Haematoxylon campechianum,* from which a
red dye is extracted. This forest's canopy attains a height of
only 8 meters (26 feet), with the logwood forming impene-
trable thickets (Figure 10). It is interesting to note that a number of species appear to be largely limited in their distribution
in central Petén to the tintal forest. It is of further interest that
most of these species are typically considered "Yucatán spe-
cialties" and reach their southern limit here. These include
the Yucatan Flycatcher, Yucatan Jay, and Rose-throated Tanager. These species may prefer this low-thicket habitat because
of its resemblance to the drier scrub forest of the Yucatán Peninsula. The Buff-bellied Hummingbird, Gray-throated Chat,
and Mangrove Vireo are also primarily restricted to the tintal
forest in central Petén.

Figure 6. Typical wide trail through the tall open forest in the central portions of Tikal National Park. Note the unexcavated ruin mound to the left of the trail. (Photograph by J. L. Tveten)

Figure 7. A healthy forest habitat is maintained adjacent to most ruin sites, as shown here near the Central Acropolis. Time should be spent birding the productive forest edge around the ruins. (Photograph by J. L. Tveten)

Figure 8. Temple IV emerges high above the tall forest. Those willing to climb this ruin will be rewarded with spectacular views above the forest canopy. (Photograph by J. L. Tveten)

Figure 9. The escobal palm forest is dominated by the palm *Cryoso-phila argentea*. This particular palm forest is located along the trail past the end of the airstrip. Note the size of these mature palms, as indicated by the people in the photograph. (Photograph by J. L. Tveten)

Figure 10. The logwood tree, *Haematoxylon campechianum*, is the dominant plant of the tintal forest. The extremely dense understory and the 7–8 meter (23–26 feet) canopy are typical features of this unique habitat. (Photograph by J. L. Tveten)

Checklist Explanatory Notes

This checklist presents 404 species of birds that have been reported from Petén. At least 352 of these species have been found within Tikal National Park. Of the total list, 250 species are residents, 6 are summer residents, 88 are winter residents or transients, and 60 are visitors. "Visitor" here refers to species that are thought to breed outside the checklist area and that do not occur regularly as transients or winter residents (see appendix 1 for a list of species by status with annotations to those reported from the park). Future studies will likely prove a number of these visitors to be regular transients or, in some cases, residents. The information presented in the checklist is based on specimen records and reliable sight records that have been supported by photographs, sketches, sound recordings, and/or detailed observation notes (see appendixes 2 and 3 for lists of species based on specimen or sight records).

Twenty species (and two forms) are presented as hypotheticals at the end of the checklist. This list includes some early records reported in Van Tyne (1935), Taibel (1955), Smithe (1966), and Land (1970). Assigning certain species to the hypothetical list is not meant to cast doubt on the credibility of observers. In recognizing the important role sight records can play in the development of a complete bird list, the author has merely chosen a conservative approach so that a more broadly accepted account could be realized. Each sight record was tested against certain criteria, including the completeness of the description, the degree of difficulty in identifying the species, the existence of additional records that support the

Figure 11. The Black Vulture, *Coragyps atratus*, has become menacingly abundant in Tikal. The Peregrine Fund attributes the abandonment of nesting in the major temples by the Orange-breasted Falcon, *Falco deiroleucus*, to the Black Vulture's use of the falcon's nesting cavities for roosting. It has been suggested that increased park attendance and a subsequent garbage problem have contributed to the increased numbers of Black Vultures in the park. (Photograph by J. L. Tveten)

Figure 12. The Roadside Hawk, *Buteo magnirostris*, is by far the most common raptor both inside and outside the park. The hawk can regularly be seen perched along the Tikal airstrip. (Photograph by J. L. Tveten)

Figure 13. The Laughing Falcon, *Herpetotheres cachinnans,* is typically found perched in the open cultivated areas outside the park. In Tikal, this falcon is occasionally seen flying overhead or perched near clearings. (Photograph by J. L. Tveten)

Figure 14. The Barred Antshrike, *Thamnophilus doliatus,* is the most widespread Formicariid in Petén and can be found anywhere there is appropriate cover. Most easily detected by its distinctive song. (Photograph by J. L. Tveten)

Figure 15. The Brown Jay (white-tipped form), *Cyanocorax morio*, is one of the most vocal birds of Petén. Nowhere can one escape the raucous calls of this conspicuous bird. (Photograph by J. L. Tveten)

Figure 16. The Montezuma Oropendola, *Psarocolius montezuma*, is a colonial nester, producing elaborate woven nests up to four feet long. The Giant Cowbird, *Scaphidura oryzivora*, can sometimes be found near these colonial nests, as it is a parasitic nester on the oropendola. (Photograph by J. L. Tveten)

occurrence of the species, and the author's knowledge of the observer's previous experience with the species. The lack of or an uncertainty in any one of the criteria usually resulted in placement on the hypothetical list. There is little doubt that additional documentation on some of these species will eventually confirm their occurrence in Petén.

Over the last thirty years, since Frank B. Smithe's extensive field work (Smithe 1966), the birdlife of Tikal has experienced many changes. The relative abundance of some species has increased, while that of others has unfortunately decreased. Of the 404 species reported from Petén, 25 have not been found in recent years (i.e., not since at least 1967); however, many of these probably still occur. A selective list of 20 species not yet reported from the region that might be expected to occur are presented at the end of the checklist as species of "Uncertain Status." These species should be carefully looked for particularly in southern Petén.

I do not present this checklist as an exhaustive and absolute account of all the birds that presently occur in Petén; nor do I expect the status that has been assigned to each species to be the final determination of their relative abundance and occurrence. Quite the contrary, this checklist merely represents the beginning of a consolidated effort to record and monitor continually the birdlife of this rich tropical region. As we have witnessed in the past, the birdlife of Petén will undoubtedly experience additional changes in years to come.

If you would like to assist in this endeavor during your stays in Tikal, carefully record your bird observations and submit them to:

Randy Beavers   Randy Beavers
c/o Jungle Lodge-Tikal   OR   Science Center
Petén, Guatemala, CA   8856 Westview Drive
                                                      Houston TX 77055, USA

Please note that reports of species not previously recorded from this region, or species indicated as "Straggler," "Hypothetical," or of "Uncertain Status" should be supported by detailed field notes on the form provided in this checklist. Observers are also encouraged to help provide additional documentation of species represented only by sight records with thorough observation notes and, if possible, photographs, sketches, and/or sound recordings of their calls.

The family names, common names, and the order in which they are presented in this checklist follow that used by the American Ornithologists' Union (1983, 1985, 1987, 1989, 1991). Each species name is followed by special codes that indicate habitat preference(s), nesting, population, and behavioral characteristics, if applicable, and then by a relative-abundance bar graph for the entire year. Each month is divided into four one-week periods for greater detail (i.e., 1–7, 8–14, 15–21, and 22–end of month). The bar graph checklist is followed by a supplemental species account that provides a detailed report of 116 Petén species not discussed in Smithe (1966), including some of the species assigned as hypotheticals by the author.

The relative-abundance indices used in the bar graph are not presented as an estimate of the actual population sizes, but rather as an indication of how often each species might be encountered in the appropriate habitat(s) and season(s). The relative abundance of some species may appear to differ from those indices assigned by the author during certain times of the year. Many of these apparent differences can be attributed to various behavioral factors that affect the degree of visibility of birds (i.e., nesting and courtship activity, frequency of vocalization, local movement patterns, and seasonal feeding patterns) and should not be interpreted as changes in their overall relative abundance.

Prefix Codes

These codes appear in Checklist, Species Account, and Appendixes.

.   Species was reported by Smithe (1966) but has not been found in recent years.

..   Species was reported by authors other than Smithe but has not been found in recent years. Some publication sources do not provide dates for certain records (e.g., Salvin and Godman 1879–1904; Land 1970), and therefore no specific records are indicated in the monthly columns for some of these species.

@   Indicates a species known only from the extreme southern portions of Petén, one to be looked for in other regions of the department. Includes the Rio de la Pasión and Rio Salinas areas in southwestern Petén and the pine ridges in southeastern Petén. Habitat codes are not provided for these marginal range species.

Habitat Codes

In the checklist, habitat codes are presented in order of preference by each species.

1   Open tall forest. A mature forest with open or rather open understory (Figure 6).

2   Dense tall forest. A forest with a rather dense understory, perhaps slightly less in canopy height and maturity than the open tall forest. Includes tall, rather mature second-growth forests.

3   Forest edges, such as found along the park's forest trails, ruin sites, parts of the airstrip, and heavily wooded roadsides (Figures 7, 8).

4   Open or rather open areas. Includes most open roadsides and fragmented forests outside the park, rather open second-growth forests, clearings, grassy fields with scattered trees, abandoned milpas, rural villages, Tikal lodge and village areas, and the hilly areas and savannas south and southwest of Lago Petén-Itzá (Figures 1, 2, 5).

5   Most often seen flying overhead. Used in reference to species rarely seen perched and apt to be observed soaring or flying over a variety of habitats (e.g., some hawks, vultures, swifts, and nighthawks).

6   Thickets, either in or near forests or adjacent to clearings.

7   Bajos and low forests. Poorly drained areas that flood seasonally. Includes the wetlands of western

Petén, escobal palm forest (Figure 9), and the unique tintal forest (Figure 10).

8   Lago Petén-Itzá and environs. Includes the inlets, lagoons, and areas immediately adjacent to the lake (Figure 3).

9   In and/or typically associated with aguadas (small ponds) throughout the checklist area (Figure 4).

10   Intermittent streams and remnant riparian woodlands, as found in the Yaxhá-Nakun-Naranjo area east toward Belize.

+   Can be found in more than three of the above habitats.

Additional Codes
(Nesting, Behavioral, Etc.)

L   Localized. A species normally found only in specific habitats or localities. Can be locally common to locally very rare.

o   Sight record only. Accepted on the basis of a reliable photograph, sketch, sound recording, or detailed observation notes; no specimen record available (see appendix 3 for complete list).

n   Known or probable nester in checklist area.

g   Often gregarious and seen in flocks of the same species in various numbers.

s   Often found in association with mixed-species
            flocks and/or ant-swarm flocks.

>   Population has significantly increased since
            Smithe's (1966) work.

<   Population has significantly decreased since
            Smithe's (1966) work.

*   Secretive and/or often difficult to see because of
            habitat or behavior.

Relative-Abundance and Occurrence Codes Used in Bar Graph Section

Common: Can be seen or heard daily in proper habitat and season.

Fairly common: Can be seen or heard most of the time (i.e., 50% or more of the time but usually not daily) in proper habitat and season.

xxxxxxxx **Uncommon:** Usually seen or heard less than 50% but more than 10% of the time in proper habitat and season.

- - - - - - - - **Rare:** Usually seen or heard less than 10% of the time in proper habitat and season. Should be expected annually.

- - - - - - - - **Very rare:** Seldom recorded during the period(s) indicated. Includes, but is not limited to, marginal range residents, transients, and regular visitors out of typical habitat and/or season.

+ or ✕   **Straggler or vagrant** (+ = post-1966 record;
            ✕ = pre-1967 record): A very seldom recorded ir-
            regular visitor or accidental species. Occurrence is
            out of normal range and is not expected annually
            (habitat codes are not provided for straggler
            species).

?   Uncertain of occurrence in the specified period(s).
            Suggests probable occurrence and should be
            looked for.

The Checklist

Quick Key to Checklist Codes

Prefix

.	Unreported in recent years (previously reported in Smithe 1966)
..	Unreported in recent years (previously reported in others)
@	Reported only from extreme southeastern or southwestern Petén

Habitat

1	Open tall forest
2	Dense tall forest
3	Forest edge
4	Open areas, open second growth, savanna
5	Flying overhead
6	Thickets
7	Bajos (low forests)
8	Lago Petén-Itzá

9	Aguadas
10	Intermittent streams, riparian woodlands
+	More than three habitats

Additional
L	Localized
o	Sight record only
n	Nester, probable nester
g	Gregarious
s	Mixed-species or ant-swarm flocks
>	More abundant since Smithe 1966
<	Less abundant since Smithe 1966
*	Secretive/difficult to see

Relative Abundance/Occurrence
▬▬▬▬	Common
(shaded)	Fairly common
xxxxxxxx	Uncommon
--------	Rare
- - - - - - - -	Very rare
+	Straggler/vagrant (post-1966)
×	Straggler/vagrant (pre-1967)
?	Uncertain occurrence (probable)

SPECIES	CODES	JAN	FEB	MAR	APR	MAY	JUN	JUL	AUG	SEP	OCT	NOV	DEC
TINAMIDAE													
Great Tinamou — *Tinamus major*	1,n,*	‖	‖	‖	‖	‖	‖	‖	‖	‖	‖	‖	‖
Little Tinamou — *Crypturellus soui*	4,6,L,n,*	‖	‖	‖	‖	‖	‖	‖	‖	‖	‖	‖	‖
Thicket Tinamou — *Crypturellus cinnamomeus*	6,2,n,*	‖	‖	‖	‖	‖	‖	‖	‖	‖	‖	‖	‖
Slaty-breasted Tinamou — *Crypturellus boucardi*	2,7,6,n,*	‖	‖	‖	‖	‖	‖	‖	‖	‖	‖	‖	‖
PODICIPEDIDAE													
Pied-billed Grebe — *Podilymbus podiceps*	8,9		‖										
Least Grebe — *Tachybaptus dominicus*	9,8,L,n								‖				
PELECANIDAE													
Brown Pelican — *Pelecanus occidentalis*	8,L,o	–	–	–	–	–	–	–	–	–	–	–	–
PHALACROCORACIDAE													
Neotropic Cormorant — *Phalacrocorax brasilianus*	8,9,L,n	–	–	–	–	–	–	–	–	–	–	–	–
ANHINGIDAE													
Anhinga — *Anhinga anhinga*	8,9,n	X	X	X	X	X	X	X	X	X	X	X	X
ARDEIDAE													
Pinnated Bittern — *Botaurus pinnatus*	o												
American Bittern — *Botaurus lentiginosus*	o						no	date					
Least Bittern — *Ixobrychus exilis*	o	+	+				+						
Bare-throated Tiger-Heron — *Tigrisoma mexicanum*	9,8,n,*	–	–	–	–	–	–	–	–	–	–	–	–
Great Blue Heron — *Ardea herodias*	9,8,o	–	–	–	–							–	–
Great Egret — *Casmerodius albus*	9,8,10	–	–	–	–							–	–
Snowy Egret — *Egretta thula*	9,8,o	–	–	–	–							–	–
Little Blue Heron — *Egretta caerulea*	9,8,10,L,<	X	X	X	X				X	X	X	+ X	X
Tricolored Heron — *Egretta tricolor*	9,8,o	–	–	–	–							–	–
Reddish Egret — *Egretta rufescens*	o			×									
Cattle Egret — *Bubulcus ibis*	4,9,8,n,>	X	X	X	X	X	X	X	X	X	X	X	X
Green-backed Heron — *Butorides striatus*	9,8,10	X	X	X	X	X	X	‖	X	X	X	X	X
@ Chestnut-bellied Heron						one	1874	record					
Black-crowned Night-Heron — *Nycticorax nycticorax*													
Yellow-crowned Night-Heron — *Nyctanassa violacea*	9,8								‖			+	
Boat-billed Heron — *Cochlearius cochlearius*	9,10,L,n,*	–	–	–	–	–	–	–	–	–	–	–	–

SPECIES		CODES	JAN	FEB	MAR	APR	MAY	JUN	JUL	AUG	SEP	OCT	NOV	DEC
THRESKIORNITHIDAE														
White Ibis	Eudocimus albus	o				+								
CICONIIDAE														
Jabiru	Jabiru mycteria	o	+	+ +	+									
Wood Stork	Mycteria americana	8,9,5,o	- -	- -	- -	-				+ +				-
ANATIDAE														
@ Black-bellied Whistling-Duck	Dendrocygna autumnalis	o	‖ ‖	‖ ‖	‖ ‖									‖
Muscovy Duck	Cairina moschata	8,L,n	‖ ‖	‖ ‖	‖ ‖	-								‖
Blue-winged Teal	Anas discors	8,9,o	‖ ‖	‖ ‖	‖ -	-								‖
Northern Shoveler	Anas clypeata	o	‖	+ +										
Ring-necked Duck	Aythya collaris	o	‖									- -		
CATHARTIDAE														
Black Vulture	Coragyps atratus	+,o,n,g,>	▓	X X X X	X X X X	X X X X	X X X	X X X	X X X	X X X	X X X	X X X	X X X	X X X
Turkey Vulture	Cathartes aura	5,4,o,	X X X	X X X	X X X +	X X X	X X X	X X X	X X X	X X X	X X X	X X X	X X X	X X X
Lesser Yellow-headed Vulture	Cathartes burrovianus	o						no	date					
King Vulture	Sarcoramphus papa	5,4,n												
ACCIPITRIDAE														
Osprey	Pandion haliaetus	8,5,L,o	- -	- -	- -	- -	▓	▓	▓	- -	- -	- -	- -	- -
Gray-headed Kite	Leptodon cayanensis	4,5,o,n	- -	- -	- -	- -	‖	‖	‖	- -	- -	- -	- -	- -
Hook-billed Kite	Chondrohierax uncinatus	4,9,8,n	- -	- -	- -	- -	‖	‖	‖	- -	- -	- -	- -	- -
American Swallow-tailed Kite	Elanoides forficatus	+,n	-	- - ‖	X X X X	X X X X	X X X	X X X	X X ‖	-				
Black-shouldered Kite	Elanus caeruleus	4,5,o,n,>	- -	- -	- -	‖	‖	‖	‖	-	- -	- -	- -	- -
Snail Kite	Rostrhamus sociabilis	8,9,L	- -	- -	- -	- -	‖	‖	‖	- -	- -	- -	- -	- -
Double-toothed Kite	Harpagus bidentatus	1,5,n	‖	‖	‖	‖	‖	‖	‖	‖	‖	‖	‖	‖
Plumbeous Kite	Ictinia plumbea	+,n			‖	X X X X	X X X	X X X	‖					
Sharp-shinned Hawk	Accipiter striatus	o	‖	+ +										‖
Bicolored Hawk	Accipiter bicolor	2,1,5,n	‖	‖	‖	‖	‖	‖	‖	‖	‖	‖	‖	‖
Crane Hawk	Geranospiza caerulescens	+,n	‖	‖	‖	‖	‖	+	‖	‖	‖	‖	‖	‖
White Hawk	Leucopternis albicollis	+,n	‖	‖	‖	‖	‖	‖	‖	‖	‖	‖	‖	‖
Common Black-Hawk	Buteogallus anthracinus	o	+	+ +	X								+	
Great Black-Hawk	Buteogallus urubitinga	+,n	‖	+ +	‖	‖	‖	‖	‖	‖	‖	‖	‖	‖

SPECIES		CODES
Black-collared Hawk	*Busarellus nigricollis*	8,7,L,n
Gray Hawk	*Buteo nitidus*	3,4,5,n
Roadside Hawk	*Buteo magnirostris*	3,4,5,n
Broad-winged Hawk	*Buteo platypterus*	5
Short-tailed Hawk	*Buteo brachyurus*	4,5,o,n
Zone-tailed Hawk	*Buteo albonotatus*	4,5,o
Crested Eagle	*Morphnus guianensis*	1,2,5,n
Black-and-white Hawk-Eagle	*Spizastur melanoleucus*	4,5,o,n
Black Hawk-Eagle	*Spizaetus tyrannus*	1,2,5,n
Ornate Hawk-Eagle	*Spizaetus ornatus*	1,2,n,*
FALCONIDAE		
Laughing Falcon	*Herpetotheres cachinnans*	4,1,n
Barred Forest-Falcon	*Micrastur ruficollis*	1,2,3,n
Collared Forest-Falcon	*Micrastur semitorquatus*	2,1,n,*
American Kestrel	*Falco sparverius*	4
Bat Falcon	*Falco rufigularis*	4,9,3,n
Orange-breasted Falcon	*Falco deiroleucus*	4,3,L,n,<
CRACIDAE		
Plain Chachalaca	*Ortalis vetula*	+,n,g
Crested Guan	*Penelope purpurascens*	3,1,2,n
Great Curassow	*Crax rubra*	2,1,n,<,*
PHASIANIDAE		
Ocellated Turkey	*Agriocharis ocellata*	+,n,g
Spotted Wood-Quail	*Odontophorus guttatus*	3,1,n,<,*
Singing Quail	*Dactylortyx thoracicus*	6,n,g,<,*
Black-throated Bobwhite	*Colinus nigrogularis*	4,L,n
RALLIDAE		
Ruddy Crake	*Laterallus ruber*	9,8,n,*
Gray-necked Wood-Rail	*Aramides cajanea*	9,L,n
Sora	*Porzana carolina*	9,L,o
Purple Gallinule	*Porphyrula martinica*	9,8,L,n

SPECIES	CODES	JAN	FEB	MAR	APR	MAY	JUN	JUL	AUG	SEP	OCT	NOV	DEC
Common Moorhen *Gallinula chloropus*	9,8,o,>	XXXX	XXXXXXX								X	XXXXX	XXXXXXXX
American Coot *Fulica americana*	8,L	- - - -	- - -										- - -
HELIORNITHIDAE													
Sungrebe *Heliornis fulica*	9,L,n	-			-								-
ARAMIDAE													
Limpkin *Aramus guarauna*	9,L,n	==	==	==	==	==	==	==	==	==	==	==	==
CHARADRIIDAE													
@ Collared Plover *Charadrius collaris*	L,o,n	==	==	==	==	==	==	==	==	==	==	==	==
Snowy Plover *Charadrius alexandrinus*	o		+		+								
. Semipalmated Plover *Charadrius semipalmatus*	4,8,9								X				
Killdeer *Charadrius vociferus*	4,8,9				==						==		
RECURVIROSTRIDAE													
Black-necked Stilt *Himantopus mexicanus*	8,9,10		- -							- -			
American Avocet *Recurvirostra americana*	o		+									+	
JACANIDAE													
Northern Jacana *Jacana spinosa*	8,9,L,n	==	==	==	==	==	==	==	==	==	==	==	==
SCOLOPACIDAE													
Greater Yellowlegs *Tringa melanoleuca*	8,9,o	- -	- -	- -	- -	- -				?	?		
Lesser Yellowlegs *Tringa flavipes*	8,9	- -	- -	- -	- -					-			
Solitary Sandpiper *Tringa solitaria*	8,9	- -	- -	- -	- -	- -			- -	- -			
Spotted Sandpiper *Actitis macularia*	8,9,10			XXXX					==	XXXXXXX			
. Upland Sandpiper *Bartramia longicauda*					X								
Western Sandpiper *Calidris mauri*	o												
Least Sandpiper *Calidris minutilla*	8,9,o										+		
. White-rumped Sandpiper *Calidris fuscicollis*						X							
Pectoral Sandpiper *Calidris melanotos*	8,9		- -		- -					- -			
Stilt Sandpiper *Calidris himantopus*	o			+									
Common Snipe *Gallinago gallinago*	8,4,9,o	- -	-							- -	- -		
Wilson's Phalarope *Phalaropus tricolor*	o				+								

SPECIES	CODES	JAN	FEB	MAR	APR	MAY	JUN	JUL	AUG	SEP	OCT	NOV	DEC
LARIDAE													
Laughing Gull — *Larus atricilla*	8,0	–	–	–								X	X
Ring-billed Gull — *Larus delawarensis*	0		+										
Royal Tern — *Sterna maxima*	8,0	–	–	+									
COLUMBIDAE													
Rock Dove — *Columba livia*	4,L,o,n,>	–	–	–	–	–	–	–	–	–	–	–	–
Pale-vented Pigeon — *Columba cayennensis*	3,4,n	X	X	X	X	X	X	X	X	X	X	X	X
Scaled Pigeon — *Columba speciosa*	4,7,3,n,*	X	X	X	X	X	X	X	X	X	X	X	X
Red-billed Pigeon — *Columba flavirostris*	4,0,n	▒	▒	▒	▒	▒	▒	▒	▒	▒	▒	▒	▒
Short-billed Pigeon — *Columba nigrirostris*	1,2,3,n	X	X	X	X	X	X	X	X	X	X	X	X
Mourning Dove — *Zenaida macroura*	4,0	–	+	+								+	–
Inca Dove — *Columbina inca*		‖	‖	‖	‖	‖	‖	‖	‖	‖	‖	‖	‖
Plain-breasted Ground-Dove — *Columbina minuta*	4,n,>	‖	‖	‖	‖	‖	‖	‖	‖	‖	‖	‖	‖
Ruddy Ground-Dove — *Columbina talpacoti*	4,7,n	█	█	█	█	█	█	█	█	█	█	█	█
Blue Ground-Dove — *Claravis pretiosa*	4,3,7,n	‖	‖	‖	‖	‖	‖	‖	‖	‖	‖	‖	‖
White-tipped Dove — *Leptotila verreauxi*	4,3,L,n	‖	‖	‖	‖	‖	‖	‖	‖	‖	‖	‖	‖
Gray-fronted Dove — *Leptotila rufaxilla*	2,1,3,n,*	‖	‖	‖	‖	‖	‖	‖	‖	‖	‖	‖	‖
Ruddy Quail-Dove — *Geotrygon montana*	2,3,7,n,*	‖	‖	‖	‖	‖	‖	‖	‖	‖	‖	‖	‖
PSITTACIDAE													
Scarlet Macaw — *Ara macao*	2,7,n	–	–	–	–	–	–	–	–	–	–	X	X
Olive-throated Parakeet — *Aratinga nana*	4,3,5,n,g	X	X	X	X	X	X	X	X	X	X	X	X
Brown-hooded Parrot — *Pionopsitta haematotis*	1,2,3,n	X	X	X	X	X	X	X	X	X	X	X	X
White-crowned Parrot — *Pionus senilis*	+,n,g	X	X	X	X	X	X	X	X	X	X	X	X
White-fronted Parrot — *Amazona albifrons*	+,n,g	X	X	X	X	X	X	X	X	X	X	X	X
Red-lored Parrot — *Amazona autumnalis*	+,n,g	X	X	X	X	X	X	X	X	X	X	X	X
Mealy Parrot — *Amazona farinosa*	1,3,4,n	█	█	█	█	█	█	█	█	█	█	█	█
CUCULIDAE													
Black-billed Cuckoo — *Coccyzus erythropthalmus*	0												
Yellow-billed Cuckoo — *Coccyzus americanus*	0				+								
Squirrel Cuckoo — *Piaya cayana*	3,2,4,n,*	X	X	X	X	X	X	X	X	X	X	X	X
Striped Cuckoo — *Tapera naevia*	4,L,o,n,>,*	X	X	X	X	+	+	+	+	X	X	X	X
Pheasant Cuckoo — *Dromococcyx phasianellus*	6,3,n,*	X	X	X	X	X	X	X	X	X	X	X	X
Groove-billed Ani — *Crotophaga sulcirostris*	4,9,n,g	X	X	X	X	X	X	X	X	X	X	X	X

SPECIES	CODES	JAN	FEB	MAR	APR	MAY	JUN	JUL	AUG	SEP	OCT	NOV	DEC
TYTONIDAE													
Barn Owl — *Tyto alba*							x						
STRIGIDAE													
Vermiculated Screech-Owl — *Otus guatemalae*	3,2,n	‖	‖	‖	‖	‖	‖	‖	‖	‖	‖	‖	‖
Spectacled Owl — *Pulsatrix perspicillata*	2,3	-	-	-	-	-	-	-	-	-	-	-	-
Ferruginous Pygmy-Owl — *Glaucidium brasilianum*	3,4,o,n,>	‖	‖	‖	‖	‖	‖	‖	‖	‖	‖	‖	‖
Mottled Owl — *Ciccaba virgata*	3,1,4,n	X	X	X	X	X	X	X	X	X	X	X	X
Black-and-white Owl — *Ciccaba nigrolineata*	3,9,2,n	‖	‖	‖	‖	‖	‖	‖	‖	‖	‖	‖	‖
CAPRIMULGIDAE													
Lesser Nighthawk — *Chordeiles acutipennis*	4,5,o	-	-	-	-					-	-		
Common Nighthawk — *Chordeiles minor*	4,5,o			-	-					-	-		
Pauraque — *Nyctidromus albicollis*	4,n	X	X	X	X	X	X	X	X	X	X	X	X
Yucatan Poorwill — *Nyctiphrynus yucatanicus*	4,3,n	X	X	X	X	X	X	X	X	X	X	X	X
Chuck-will's-widow — *Caprimulgus carolinensis*											x		
NYCTIBIIDAE													
@ .Great Potoo — *Nyctibius grandis*		-	-	-	-	-	-	-	-	-	-	-	-
Common Potoo — *Nyctibius griseus*	10,9,4,L,n	-	-	-						-	-	-	-
APODIDAE													
White-collared Swift — *Streptoprocne zonaris*	4,5,o	-	-	-								-	-
Chimney Swift — *Chaetura pelagica*	o				+								
Vaux's Swift — *Chaetura vauxi*	5,4,n,g	X	X	X	X	X	X	X	X	X	X	X	X
Lesser Swallow-tailed Swift — *Panyptila cayennensis*	5,4,o,n	X	X	X	X	X	X	X	X	X	X	X	X
TROCHILIDAE													
Long-tailed Hermit — *Phaethornis superciliosus*	3,2,4,n	X	X	X	X	X	X	X	X	X	X	X	X
Little Hermit — *Phaethornis longuemareus*	3,2,4,n	X	X	X	X	X	X	X	X	X	X	X	X
Scaly-breasted Hummingbird — *Phaeochroa cuvierii*	3,2,4,n	‖	‖	‖	‖	‖	‖	‖	‖	‖	‖	‖	‖
Wedge-tailed Sabrewing — *Campylopterus curvipennis*	3,n,<	‖	‖	‖	‖	‖	‖	‖	‖	‖	‖	‖	‖
White-necked Jacobin — *Florisuga mellivora*	1,2,3,n	‖	‖	‖	‖	‖	‖	‖	‖	‖	‖	‖	‖
Green-breasted Mango — *Anthracothorax prevostii*	3,1,4,n	X	X	X	X	X	X	X	X	X	X	X	X
Black-crested Coquette — *Lophornis helenae*	3,7,o	-	-	-									-

SPECIES		CODES	JAN	FEB	MAR	APR	MAY	JUN	JUL	AUG	SEP	OCT	NOV	DEC
Fork-tailed Emerald	Chlorostilbon canivetii	3,4,6,n	X	X	X	X	X	X	X	X	X	X	X	X
White-bellied Emerald	Amazilia candida	1,2,3,n	X	X	X	X	X	X	X	X	X	X	X	X
Azure-crowned Hummingbird	Amazilia cyanocephala	4,3,n	‖	‖	x	+	‖	‖	‖	‖	‖	‖	‖	‖
Rufous-tailed Hummingbird	Amazilia tzacatl		X	X	X	X	X	X	X	X	X	X	X	X
Buff-bellied Hummingbird	Amazilia yucatanensis	7,6,n	‖	‖	‖	‖	‖	‖	‖	‖	‖	‖	‖	‖
@..Stripe-tailed Hummingbird	Eupherusa eximia							no date						
Purple-crowned Fairy	Heliothryx barroti	3,1,n	‖	‖	‖						‖	‖		‖
Ruby-throated Hummingbird	Archilochus colubris	3,4				x								
..Long-billed Starthroat	Heliomaster longirostris													
TROGONIDAE														
Black-headed Trogon	Trogon melanocephalus	3,1,4,n	X	X	X	X	X	X	X	X	X	X	X	X
Violaceous Trogon	Trogon violaceus	3,4,n,>	X	X	X	X	X	X	X	X	X	X	X	X
Collared Trogon	Trogon collaris	1,3,n,*	X	X	X	X	X	X	X	X	X	X	X	X
Slaty-tailed Trogon	Trogon massena	3,2,4,n	X	X	X	X	X	X	X	X	X	X	X	X
MOMOTIDAE														
Tody Motmot	Hylomanes momotula	6,2,7,n,*												
Blue-crowned Motmot	Momotus momota	1,3,2,n,*	X	X	X	X	X	X	X	X	X	X	X	X
Keel-billed Motmot	Electron carinatum	o						x						
ALCEDINIDAE														
Ringed Kingfisher	Ceryle torquata	9,8,L,n	‖	‖	‖	‖	‖	‖	‖	‖	‖	‖	‖	‖
Belted Kingfisher	Ceryle alcyon	9,L	--	--	--						--	--	--	--
Amazon Kingfisher	Chloroceryle amazona	10,9,L	‖	‖	‖	‖						‖	‖	‖
Green Kingfisher	Chloroceryle americana	9,8,10,L,n	‖	‖	‖	‖	‖	‖	‖	‖	‖	‖	‖	‖
American Pygmy Kingfisher	Chloroceryle aenea	9,10,L,n	‖	‖	‖	‖								
BUCCONIDAE														
White-necked Puffbird	Bucco macrorhynchos	3,9,n,*	‖	‖	‖	‖	‖	‖	‖	‖	‖	‖	‖	‖
White-whiskered Puffbird	Malacoptila panamensis	2,6,3,n,*												
GALBULIDAE														
Rufous-tailed Jacamar	Galbula ruficauda	2,3,n												

SPECIES	CODES	JAN	FEB	MAR	APR	MAY	JUN	JUL	AUG	SEP	OCT	NOV	DEC
RAMPHASTIDAE													
Emerald Toucanet — *Aulacorhynchus prasinus*	1,3,n,*	X	X	X	X	X	X	X	X	X	X	X	X
Collared Aracari — *Pteroglossus torquatus*	+,n,g	X	X	X	X	X	X	X	X	X	X	X	X
Keel-billed Toucan — *Ramphastos sulfuratus*	+,n	X	X	X	X	X	X	X	X	X	X	X	X
PICIDAE													
. Acorn Woodpecker — *Melanerpes formicivorus*													
Black-cheeked Woodpecker — *Melanerpes pucherani*	4,3,n	X	X	X	X	X	X	X	X	X	X	X	X
Golden-fronted Woodpecker — *Melanerpes aurifrons*	4,3,n,>	X	X	X	X	X	X	X	X	X	X	X	X
Yellow-bellied Sapsucker — *Sphyrapicus varius*			+ +	X				X					
Smoky-brown Woodpecker — *Veniliornis fumigatus*	2,6,n,*						X						
Golden-olive Woodpecker — *Piculus rubiginosus*	3,2,n												
Chestnut-colored Woodpecker — *Celeus castaneus*	2,3,n												
Lineated Woodpecker — *Dryocopus lineatus*	3,4,n	X	X	X	X	X	X	X	X	X	X	X	X
Pale-billed Woodpecker — *Campephilus guatemalensis*	1,3,4,n	X	X	X	X	X	X	X	X	X	X	X	X
FURNARIIDAE													
Rufous-breasted Spinetail — *Synallaxis erythrothorax*	4,L,o,n,>,*	=	=	=	=	X	X	X	X	X	X	X	=
Buff-throated Foliage-gleaner — *Automolus ochrolaemus*	6,7,2,n,*	=	=	=	=	X	X	X	X	X	X	X	X
Plain Xenops — *Xenops minutus*	1,2,3,n,s	=	=	=	X	X	X	X	X	X	X	X	X
Scaly-throated Leaftosser — *Sclerurus guatemalensis*	1,n,*	=	=	=	X	X	X	X	X	X	X	X	X
DENDROCOLAPTIDAE													
Tawny-winged Woodcreeper — *Dendrocincla anabatina*	3,1,2,n	X	X	X	X	X	X	X	X	X	X	X	X
Ruddy Woodcreeper — *Dendrocincla homochroa*	3,2,1,n,s	X	X	X	X	X	X	X	X	X	X	X	X
Olivaceous Woodcreeper — *Sittasomus griseicapillus*	+,n,s	-	-	-	-	-	-	-	-	-	-	-	-
Wedge-billed Woodcreeper — *Glyphorynchus spirurus*	3,4,n	-	-	-	-	-	-	-	-	-	-	-	-
Strong-billed Woodcreeper — *Xiphocolaptes promeropirhynchus*	3,n												
Barred Woodcreeper — *Dendrocolaptes certhia*	3,2,n,s												
Ivory-billed Woodcreeper — *Xiphorhynchus flavigaster*	3,4,n	X	X	X	X	X	X	X	X	X	X	X	X
Streak-headed Woodcreeper — *Lepidocolaptes souleyetii*	3,2,1,n												
FORMICARIIDAE													
Great Antshrike — *Taraba major*	6,4,L,n,*	-	-	-	-	-	-	-	-	-	-	-	-
Barred Antshrike — *Thamnophilus doliatus*	4,6,3,n	X	X	X	X	X	X	X	X	X	X	X	X

SPECIES		CODES	JAN	FEB	MAR	APR	MAY	JUN	JUL	AUG	SEP	OCT	NOV	DEC
Russet Antshrike	*Thamnistes anabatinus*	2,3,n,*	X	X	X	X	X	X	X	X	X	X	X	X
Plain Antvireo	*Dysithamnus mentalis*	2,3,n	X	X	X	X	X	X	X	X	X	X	X	X
Dot-winged Antwren	*Microrhopias quixensis*	3,2,6,n,s	X	X	X	X	X	X	X	X	X	X	X	X
Dusky Antbird	*Cercomacra tyrannina*	2,6,3,n,*	X	X	X	X	X	X	X	X	X	X	X	X
Black-faced Antthrush	*Formicarius analis*	1,3,n,*	X	X	X	X	X	X	X	X	X	X	X	X
TYRANNIDAE														
Paltry Tyrannulet	*Zimmerius vilissimus*	3,4,n,*	X	X	X	X	X	X	X	X	X	X	X	X
Yellow-bellied Tyrannulet	*Ornithion semiflavum*	3,6,n												
Northern Beardless-Tyrannulet	*Camptostoma imberbe*	6,3,n												
Greenish Elaenia	*Myiopagis viridicata*	+,n												
Yellow-bellied Elaenia	*Elaenia flavogaster*	4,6,L,n												
Ochre-bellied Flycatcher	*Mionectes oleagineus*	3,1,4,n	X	X	X	X	X	X	X	X	X	X	X	X
Sepia-capped Flycatcher	*Leptopogon amaurocephalus*	2,3,n	X	X	X	X	X	X	X	X	X	X	X	X
Northern Bentbill	*Oncostoma cinereigulare*	2,3,6,n	X	X	X	X	X	X	X	X	X	X	X	X
Slate-headed Tody-Flycatcher	*Todirostrum sylvia*	6,3,n												
Common Tody-Flycatcher	*Todirostrum cinereum*	4,10,L												
Eye-ringed Flatbill	*Rhynchocyclus brevirostris*	1,3,n												
Yellow-olive Flycatcher	*Tolmomyias sulphurescens*	1,3,4,n	X	X	X	X	X	X	X	X	X	X	X	X
Stub-tailed Spadebill	*Platyrinchus cancrominus*	3,2,6,n												
Royal Flycatcher	*Onychorhynchus coronatus*	3,1,n												
Ruddy-tailed Flycatcher	*Terenotriccus erythrurus*	3,4,n												
Sulphur-rumped Flycatcher	*Myiobius sulphureipygius*	2,3,n	X	X	X	X	X	X	X	X	X	X	X	X
Olive-sided Flycatcher	*Contopus borealis*	4,3				—	—				—	—		
Greater Pewee	*Contopus pertinax*	3,4,1,o												
Eastern Wood-Pewee	*Contopus virens*	1,4	—	—							X	X		
Tropical Pewee	*Contopus cinereus*	3,4,n												
Yellow-bellied Flycatcher	*Empidonax flaviventris*	6,3	—	—	X	?	?				X	X		
Alder Flycatcher	*Empidonax alnorum*	+				?	?					X		
Willow Flycatcher	*Empidonax trailii*	6,4				?	?				X	X		
...White-throated Flycatcher	*Empidonax albigularis*	+						X						
Least Flycatcher	*Empidonax minimus*	+	—	—	—	—	—					X		
(Empidonax Flycatcher)	*Empidonax sp.*	+	—	X	X	X	—				X	X	X	X
@ - Black Phoebe	*Sayornis nigricans*	o	—	—	—	—								
Vermilion Flycatcher	*Pyrocephalus rubinus*	4,L,n				—	—						—	—

SPECIES	CODES	JAN	FEB	MAR	APR	MAY	JUN	JUL	AUG	SEP	OCT	NOV	DEC
Bright-rumped Attila	*Attila spadiceus*	░	░	░	░	░	░	░	░	░	░	░	░
Rufous Mourner	*Rhytipterna holerythra*	░	░	░	░	░	░	░	░	░	░	░	░
Yucatan Flycatcher	*Myiarchus yucatanensis*	X	X	X	X	X	X	X	X			X	X
Dusky-capped Flycatcher	*Myiarchus tuberculifer*	░	░	░	░	░	░	░	░	░	░	░	░
Great Crested Flycatcher	*Myiarchus crinitus*		X	X	X						X		
Brown-crested Flycatcher	*Myiarchus tyrannulus*	X	X	X	X	X	X				X	X	X
Great Kiskadee	*Pitangus sulphuratus*	░	░	░	░	░	░	░	░	░	░	░	░
Boat-billed Flycatcher	*Megarynchus pitangua*	░	░	░	░	░	░	░	░	░	░	░	░
Social Flycatcher	*Myiozetetes similis*	▓	▓	▓	▓	▓	▓	▓	▓	▓	▓	▓	▓
Streaked Flycatcher	*Myiodynastes maculatus*			‖	‖				‖	‖			
Sulphur-bellied Flycatcher	*Myiodynastes luteiventris*		‖	‖					‖	‖			
Piratic Flycatcher	*Legatus leucophaius*			‖						‖			
Tropical Kingbird	*Tyrannus melancholicus*	X	X	X	X	X	X	X	X	X	X	X	X
Couch's Kingbird	*Tyrannus couchii*	X	X	X	X	X	X	X	X	X	X	X	X
Eastern Kingbird	*Tyrannus tyrannus*				‖					‖	X	‖	
Scissor-tailed Flycatcher	*Tyrannus forficatus*	X	X	X	X	X	X	X	X	X	X	X	X
Fork-tailed Flycatcher	*Tyrannus savana*	‖	‖	‖	‖	‖	‖	‖	‖	‖	‖	‖	‖
Cinnamon Becard	*Pachyramphus cinnamomeus*	‖	‖	‖	‖	‖	‖	‖	‖	‖	‖	‖	‖
Gray-collared Becard	*Pachyramphus major*	X	X	X	X	X	X	X	X	X	X	X	X
Rose-throated Becard	*Pachyramphus aglaiae*	X	X	X	X	X	X	X	X	X	X	X	X
Masked Tityra	*Tityra semifasciata*	X	X	X	X	X	X	X	X	X	X	X	X
Black-crowned Tityra	*Tityra inquisitor*	X	X	X	X	X	X	X	X	X	X	X	X

COTINGIDAE

SPECIES	CODES	JAN	FEB	MAR	APR	MAY	JUN	JUL	AUG	SEP	OCT	NOV	DEC
Rufous Piha	*Lipaugus unirufus*	░	░	░	░	░	░	░	░	░	░	░	░
Lovely Cotinga	*Cotinga amabilis*	░	░	░	░	░	░	░	░	░	░	░	░

PIPRIDAE

SPECIES	CODES	JAN	FEB	MAR	APR	MAY	JUN	JUL	AUG	SEP	OCT	NOV	DEC
Thrush-like Manakin	*Schiffornis turdinus*	X	X	X	X	X	X	X	X	X	X	X	X
White-collared Manakin	*Manacus candei*	X	X	X	X	X	X	X	X	X	X	X	X
Red-capped Manakin	*Pipra mentalis*	X	X	X	X	X	X	X	X	X	X	X	X

HIRUNDINIDAE

SPECIES	CODES	JAN	FEB	MAR	APR	MAY	JUN	JUL	AUG	SEP	OCT	NOV	DEC
Purple Martin	*Progne subis*	‖	‖		‖					‖	‖		
..Sinaloa Martin	*Progne sinaloae*			x									

SPECIES		CODES	JAN	FEB	MAR	APR	MAY	JUN	JUL	AUG	SEP	OCT	NOV	DEC
Gray-breasted Martin	Progne chalybea	4,5,n,g												
Tree Swallow	Tachycineta bicolor	4,5,o												
Mangrove Swallow	Tachycineta albilinea	8,5,n,g												
Northern Rough-winged Swallow	Stelgidopteryx serripennis	4,5,n,g												
Bank Swallow	Riparia riparia	9,8,4,o												
Cliff Swallow	Hirundo pyrrhonota	o												
Barn Swallow	Hirundo rustica	4,5,8,g												
CORVIDAE														
Green Jay	Cyanocorax yncas	6,4,7,n												
Brown Jay	Cyanocorax morio	+,n,g												
Yucatan Jay	Cyanocorax yucatanicus	7,L,n,*												
TROGLODYTIDAE														
Band-backed Wren	Campylorhynchus zonatus	10,6,4,L,n												
Spot-breasted Wren	Thryothorus maculipectus	+,n												
Carolina Wren (White-browed)	Thryothorus ludovicianus	6,3,n												
House Wren (Southern)	Troglodytes aedon	3,6,n,>												
White-bellied Wren	Uropsila leucogastra	2,3,6,n												
White-breasted Wood-Wren	Henicorhina leucosticta	6,2,n												
Gray-breasted Wood-Wren	Henicorhina leucophrys							×						
@ Nightingale Wren	Microcerculus philomela	n												
MUSCICAPIDAE (Sylviinae)														
Long-billed Gnatwren	Ramphocaenus melanurus	2,3,6,n												
Blue-gray Gnatcatcher	Polioptila caerulea	4,7,3												
Tropical Gnatcatcher	Polioptila plumbea	3,1,n												
MUSCICAPIDAE (Turdinae)														
Veery	Catharus fuscescens	3,1,6												
Gray-cheeked Thrush	Catharus minimus	1,3,4												
Swainson's Thrush	Catharus ustulatus	1,3,4												
Wood Thrush	Hylocichla mustelina	1,3												
Clay-colored Robin	Turdus grayi	4,3,n												
White-throated Robin	Turdus assimilis	1,2,3,n,<												

SPECIES		CODES	JAN	FEB	MAR	APR	MAY	JUN	JUL	AUG	SEP	OCT	NOV	DEC
MIMIDAE														
Gray Catbird	*Dumetella carolinensis*	6,3,7											X	
Black Catbird	*Melanoptila glabrirostris*	4,6,3,L,n												
Tropical Mockingbird	*Mimus gilvus*	10,0												
BOMBYCILLIDAE														
Cedar Waxwing	*Bombycilla cedrorum*	4,3,9												
VIREONIDAE														
White-eyed Vireo	*Vireo griseus*	4,1,3		X X X X X	X X X X							X X X X	X X X X	X X X X
Mangrove Vireo	*Vireo pallens*	7,6,L,n	X X X X X X X	X X X X X X X	X X X X X X X	X X X X X X	X X X X X X	X X X X X X	X X X X X X	X X X X X X	X X X X X X	X X X X X X	X X X X X X	X X X X X X
Solitary Vireo	*Vireo solitarius*	3,4,1,0											X X X	X X X X
Yellow-throated Vireo	*Vireo flavifrons*	4,0												
Warbling Vireo	*Vireo gilvus*	3,4,0												
Philadelphia Vireo	*Vireo philadelphicus*	4,6												
Red-eyed Vireo	*Vireo olivaceus*	4,3			X X									
Yellow-green Vireo	*Vireo flavoviridis*	4,1,n					X X X X X X X	X X X			X X			
Tawny-crowned Greenlet	*Hylophilus ochraceiceps*	2,3,1,n,s	X X X X X X X X X X	X X X X X X X X X X	X X X X X X X X X X	X X X X X X X X X X	X X X X X X X X X X	X X X X X X X X X X	X X X X X X X X X X	X X X X X X X X X X	X X X X X X X X X X	X X X X X X X X X X	X X X X X X X X X X	X X X X X X X X X X
Lesser Greenlet	*Hylophilus decurtatus*	3,4,1,n												
Green Shrike-Vireo	*Vireolanius pulchellus*	1,3,4,n,*												
Rufous-browed Peppershrike	*Cyclarhis gujanensis*	4,L,o,n,>												
EMBERIZIDAE (Parulinae)														
Blue-winged Warbler	*Vermivora pinus*	3,4,6												
Golden-winged Warbler	*Vermivora chrysoptera*	3,4,1,0			X X X X X							X X X		
Tennessee Warbler	*Vermivora peregrina*	3,1										+		
Orange-crowned Warbler	*Vermivora celata*	0												
Nashville Warbler	*Vermivora ruficapilla*	3,0												
Northern Parula	*Parula americana*	1,3,0												
Tropical Parula	*Parula pitiayumi*	0		+		x								
Yellow Warbler	*Dendroica petechia*	4,9		X X X X X	X X X X							X X		
Chestnut-sided Warbler	*Dendroica pensylvanica*	3,4												
Magnolia Warbler	*Dendroica magnolia*	3,4	X X X X X X X	X X X X X	X X X								X X X X X X	X X X X X X
Cape May Warbler	*Dendroica tigrina*	3,4,0			X X									
Yellow-rumped Warbler (Myrtle)	*Dendroica coronata*	4												
Black-throated Green Warbler	*Dendroica virens*	1,4,3												

SPECIES		CODES	JAN	FEB	MAR	APR	MAY	JUN	JUL	AUG	SEP	OCT	NOV	DEC
Blackburnian Warbler	*Dendroica fusca*	4,3	-	-	-	-					-		-	
Yellow-throated Warbler	*Dendroica dominica*	4,1,0	-	-	-	-							-	-
Bay-breasted Warbler	*Dendroica castanea*	3,4,0	-	-	=	-								■
Cerulean Warbler	*Dendroica cerulea*										×			
Black-and-white Warbler	*Mniotilta varia*	1,3,4			×××	×××				-	×	××××	××××	■
American Redstart	*Setophaga ruticilla*	1,3,4				××	--			=		××	××××	××××
Prothonotary Warbler	*Protonotaria citrea*	9,6			-									
Worm-eating Warbler	*Helmitheros vermivorus*	2,3		××	×××								××	
Swainson's Warbler	*Limnothlypis swainsonii*	0		++										
Ovenbird	*Seiurus aurocapillus*	1,2,3	=	=	××	=						×	×	
Northern Waterthrush	*Seiurus noveboracensis*	6,9	=	=	×××	=				-	=	××××	■	■
Louisiana Waterthrush	*Seiurus motacilla*	1,3,9	=	=	×××	=			=	=	=	××	××	■
Kentucky Warbler	*Oporornis formosus*	1,2,3	×××××	××××	×××××	=				=	=	××	=	×××
Mourning Warbler	*Oporornis philadelphia*					-	××							
Common Yellowthroat	*Geothlypis trichas*	6,9,4,L	=	=	××	=					=	××	××	■
Gray-crowned Yellowthroat	*Geothlypis poliocephala*	4,8,9,L,n	=	=	×××××	=				-	=	××	=	■
Hooded Warbler	*Wilsonia citrina*	3,6	=	=	×××××	=				-	=	××	=	■
Wilson's Warbler	*Wilsonia pusilla*	6,9	=	=	=	-								■
Canada Warbler	*Wilsonia canadensis*	3,2,0			-	-					=	-	-	
Golden-crowned Warbler	*Basileuterus culicivorus*	3,1,2,n	××××××××××××××××××××××××××××××××									××××
Yellow-breasted Chat	*Icteria virens*	6,3,4	=	=	×××××	=				-	=	×××××	■	■
Gray-throated Chat	*Granatellus sallaei*	7,L,n,*								=				
EMBERIZIDAE (Coerebinae)														
Bananaquit	*Coereba flaveola*	4,3,n	=	=										■
EMBERIZIDAE (Thraupinae)														
Golden-masked Tanager	*Tangara larvata*	4,3,n,g	××××××××××××××××××××××××××××××××									××××
Green Honeycreeper	*Chlorophanes spiza*	1,4,3,n	=	=	=	=				=	=	=	=	■
Red-legged Honeycreeper	*Cyanerpes cyaneus*	1,4,3,n,g	××××××××××××××××××××××××××××××××									××××
Scrub Euphonia	*Euphonia affinis*	3,4,n,g	=	=	=	=				=	=	=	=	■
Yellow-throated Euphonia	*Euphonia hirundinacea*	4,3,n,g	××××××××××××××××××××××××××××××××									××××
Olive-backed Euphonia	*Euphonia gouldi*	4,3,2,n,s	××××××××××××××××××××××××××××××××									××××
Blue-gray Tanager	*Thraupis episcopus*	4,n	=	=	=	=				=	=	=	=	■
Yellow-winged Tanager	*Thraupis abbas*	4,3,n,g	××××××××××××××××××××××××××××××××									××××
Gray-headed Tanager	*Eucometis penicillata*	3,2,n,s	××××××××××××××××××××××××××××××××									××××

SPECIES	CODES	JAN	FEB	MAR	APR	MAY	JUN	JUL	AUG	SEP	OCT	NOV	DEC
Black-throated Shrike-Tanager	*Lanio aurantius*	2,3,n,s											
Red-crowned Ant-Tanager	*Habia rubica*	2,1,n,s											
Red-throated Ant-Tanager	*Habia fuscicauda*	2,3,1,n,s											
Rose-throated Tanager	*Piranga roseogularis*	7,3,L,n											
Hepatic Tanager	*Piranga flava*				x +								X X X X X X X
Summer Tanager	*Piranga rubra*	4,3	X X X X X X X X X		—						—		
Scarlet Tanager	*Piranga olivacea*	3,4,0			—	—						—		
Western Tanager	*Piranga ludoviciana*	0						no						
Flame-colored Tanager	*Piranga bidentata*	3,2,n						x	date					
White-winged Tanager	*Piranga leucoptera*	4,L,n												
Crimson-collared Tanager	*Ramphocelus sanguinolentus*													
@ Scarlet-rumped Tanager	*Ramphocelus passerinii*	0												

EMBERIZIDAE (Cardinalinae)

SPECIES	CODES	JAN	FEB	MAR	APR	MAY	JUN	JUL	AUG	SEP	OCT	NOV	DEC
Grayish Saltator	*Saltator coerulescens*	4,L,n,>	X	X	X	X	X	X	X	X	X	X	X	X
Buff-throated Saltator	*Saltator maximus*	4,L,o,n,>	X	X	X	X	X	X	X	X	X	X	X	X
Black-headed Saltator	*Saltator atriceps*	3,6,4,n	X	X	X	X	X	X	X	X	X	X	X	X
Black-faced Grosbeak	*Caryothraustes poliogaster*	2,6,4,n												
Northern Cardinal	*Cardinalis cardinalis*	6,4,L,n												
Rose-breasted Grosbeak	*Pheucticus ludovicianus*	4,3			—	—						—		
Blue-black Grosbeak	*Cyanocompsa cyanoides*	6,3,4,n												
Blue Bunting	*Cyanocompsa parellina*	3,6,4,n,<												
Blue Grosbeak	*Guiraca caerulea*	4,9,3			X X X X	X X								
Indigo Bunting	*Passerina cyanea*	4,3												
Painted Bunting	*Passerina ciris*	4,6,3										X X		
Dickcissel	*Spiza americana*	4												

EMBERIZIDAE (Emberizinae)

SPECIES	CODES	JAN	FEB	MAR	APR	MAY	JUN	JUL	AUG	SEP	OCT	NOV	DEC
Orange-billed Sparrow	*Arremon aurantiirostris*	2,n,<,*												
Olive Sparrow	*Arremonops rufivirgatus*	4,<,n												
Green-backed Sparrow	*Arremonops chloronotus*	4,3,7,n												
Blue-black Grassquit	*Volatinia jacarina*	4,3,n,g												
White-collared Seedeater	*Sporophila torqueola*	4,n,g												
Thick-billed Seed-Finch	*Oryzoborus funereus*	4,6,n,g												
Yellow-faced Grassquit	*Tiaris olivacea*	4,n												

SPECIES		CODES	JAN	FEB	MAR	APR	MAY	JUN	JUL	AUG	SEP	OCT	NOV	DEC
Botteri's Sparrow	*Aimophila botterii*	8,4,L,n												
@ Rusty Sparrow	*Aimophila rufescens*	n												
@ Chipping Sparrow	*Spizella passerina*	n												
..Grasshopper Sparrow	*Ammodramus savannarum*					x					x x			
EMBERIZIDAE (Icterinae)														
.Bobolink	*Dolichonyx oryzivorus*										x x	x x		
Red-winged Blackbird	*Agelaius phoeniceus*	4,8,L,n												
Eastern Meadowlark	*Sturnella magna*	4,L,n												
Melodious Blackbird	*Dives dives*	+,n												
Great-tailed Grackle	*Quiscalus mexicanus*	4,3,n,g,>												
Bronzed Cowbird	*Molothrus aeneus*	4,L,n,g,>												
Giant Cowbird	*Scaphidura oryzivora*	4,3,n,g												
Black-cowled Oriole	*Icterus dominicensis*	3,4,n												
Orchard Oriole	*Icterus spurius*	3,4,												
Yellow-backed Oriole	*Icterus chrysater*	1,3,4,o												
Yellow-tailed Oriole	*Icterus mesomelas*	4,6,10,L,n												
Altamira Oriole	*Icterus gularis*	3,4		+										
Northern Oriole	*Icterus galbula*	3,4											+	
Yellow-billed Cacique	*Amblycercus holosericeus*	4,6,n,g									XXX	XXX		
@..Chestnut-headed Oropendola	*Psarocolius wagleri*													
Montezuma Oropendola	*Psarocolius montezuma*	+,n,g	+											
HYPOTHETICALS														
Sharp-shinned Hawk (wh-brst.)	*Accipiter s. chionogaster*	o		+										
Cooper's Hawk	*Accipiter cooperii*	o			+									
Solitary Eagle	*Harpyhaliaetus solitarius*	o			+ + +									
Gray-breasted Crake	*Laterallus exilis*	o			+									
Spotted Rail	*Pardirallus maculatus*	o		+										
Common Ground-Dove	*Columbina passerina*	o			x									
Gray-chested Dove	*Leptotila cassini*	o				+								
Yellow-lored Parrot	*Amazona xantholora*	o	+											
@..Yellow-naped Parrot	*Amazona auropalliata*	o	+											
Least Pygmy-Owl	*Glaucidium minutissimum*	o					no	date						
Beryline Hummingbird	*Amazilia beryllina*	o		+					x					
..Bare-crowned Antbird	*Gymnocichla nudiceps*	o								+				

SPECIES		CODES	JAN	FEB	MAR	APR	MAY	JUN	JUL	AUG	SEP	OCT	NOV	DEC
Acadian Flycatcher	*Empidonax virescens*	o			+									
..Dusky Flycatcher	*Empidonax oberholseri*	o?		+										
Virginia's Warbler	*Vermivora virginiae*	o	+											
Yellow-rumped Warbler (Aud.)	*Dendroica c. auduboni*	o		+										
.Townsend's Warbler	*Dendroica townsendi*	o			x x						+			
Golden-cheeked Warbler	*Dendroica chrysoparia*	o			x						+			
@ Grace's Warbler	*Dendroica graciae*	o				+								
Rufous-capped Warbler	*Basileuterus rufifrons*	o				x								
Blue-hooded Euphonia	*Euphonia elegantissima*	o		+										
.Orange Oriole	*Icterus auratus*	o			x									

UNCERTAIN STATUS *(TO BE LOOKED FOR)*

SPECIES	
White-faced Ibis	*Plegadis chihi*
Roseate Spoonbill	*Ajaia ajaja*
Masked Duck	*Oxyura dominica*
Northern Harrier	*Circus cyaneus*
Swainson's Hawk	*Buteo swainsoni*
Harpy Eagle	*Harpia harpyja*
Crested Caracara	*Polyborus plancus*
Aplomado Falcon	*Falco femoralis*
Peregrine Falcon	*Falco peregrinus*
Uniform Crake	*Amaurolimnas concolor*
Sunbittern	*Eurypyga helias*
Stygian Owl	*Asio stygius*
Tawny-collared Nightjar (Yuc.)	*Caprimulgus salvini*
Band-tailed Barbthroat	*Threnetes ruckeri*
Brown Violet-ear	*Colibri delphinae*
Crowned Woodnymph	*Thalurania columbica*
Blue-throated Goldentail	*Hylocharis eliciae*
Olivaceous Piculet	*Picumnus olivaceus*
White-vented Euphonia	*Euphonia minuta*
Variable Seedeater	*Sporophila aurita*

Supplemental Species Account

This section provides a brief account of 116 Petén species and one form (including 14 of the hypotheticals) not treated by Smithe (1966), presenting the current status in the region and the specific habitats and/or localities from which each has been reported. Species not reported since 1967 are not included in this account.

Brown Pelican　　　　*Pelecanus occidentalis*
Very rare visitor

Although most sightings have come from the Lago Petén-Itzá area, there have been occasional reports of this pelican flying overhead near Tikal National Park. The first, and only, park record was reported on 17 February 1989 by F. Oatman. This pelican has been seen practically every month in other parts of central Petén.

Pinnated Bittern　　　　*Botaurus pinnatus*
Visitor; probable rare and localized resident

A 19 November 1977 sighting of three Pinnated Bitterns at Lago Petén-Itzá by F. Oatman is the only known record from Petén (he also reported this bittern days earlier on 12 November 1977 along the Rio Dulce in Izabal). This very secretive bird should occur throughout the year along the remote shallow marshes of Lago Petén-Itzá and perhaps in western Petén.

Least Bittern   *Ixobrychus exilis*
Visitor; possible rare and localized resident

Other than an indication by Land (1970) as rare in Petén, the
only records known from this department are three sightings
at Aguada Tikal in the park: on 6 June 1957 by E. P. Edwards
et al. (pers. comm. K. Ladwig), and two records in January
1977 by C. Leahy. Should occur in suitable habitat (e.g.,
aquatic areas with cattails, sedge, etc.) throughout Petén.

Tricolored Heron   *Egretta tricolor*
Very rare winter resident

Restricted primarily to the shallows of Lago Petén-Itzá and
larger aguadas from September to April. Although Land
(1970) suggests this species is a resident here, no Petén records
from the summer period are known.

Black-crowned Night-Heron   *Nycticorax nycticorax*
Visitor at Tikal; probably more common outside the park

Land (1970) indicates this species is a rare resident in southern Petén, but there were no park records until 27 November
1976 by R. A. Rowlett. To be looked for in the more remote
aguadas throughout Petén.

White Ibis   *Eudocimus albus*
Visitor

Land (1970) indicates this species is rare in Petén. One recent
sight record was reported at Dos Lagunas north of Uaxactún
on 13 April 1990 by J. Vannini. To be looked for in the lagoons
of Lago Petén-Itzá and in the low wetlands of western Petén.

Jabiru   *Jabiru mycteria*
Visitor at Tikal; probable rare and localized resident in remote
bajos outside Tikal

Has been reported from Tikal on several occasions, including flying overhead on 7 February 1978 by F. Oatman and 4 January 1990 by J. Lyons, and along the airstrip on 2 January 1989 by C. Benesh and 2 March 1990 by S. Fisher and M. Lambarth (pers. comm. F. Oatman). Also reported from Lago Petén-Itzá on 13–16 August 1976 by C. Leahy, and near Sayaxché on 10 February 1978 by F. Oatman.

@ **Black-bellied Whistling-Duck**   *Dendrocygna autumnalis*
Rare and localized resident in southern Petén

Indicated by Land (1970) as fairly common along the Pacific coast and rare in southwestern Petén. On 2 September 1977 J. Smith reported this species from Sayaxché, where it is probably resident along the Rio de la Pasión (no definite breeding records), and S. N. G. Howell reported two near the Petén-Izabal border on 16 June 1988.

Muscovy Duck   *Cairina moschata*
Rare resident on Lago Petén-Itzá and larger wooded aguadas

First reported in Petén by Salvin and Godman (1879–1904) from Lago Petén-Itzá. More recently sighted at this lake in February 1988 by D. Delaney and again in September 1989 by R. Beavers. Also reported from Ceibal on 3 February 1969 by F. Oatman, and in southern Petén on 20 February 1973 by T. Davis (pers. comm. P. Alden). Some individuals may be of the domesticated form.

Northern Shoveler   *Anas clypeata*
Visitor (winter)

February 1978 sightings of this species (one male) at Aguada Tikal (R. A. Rowlett) and at Lago Petén-Itzá (F. Oatman) are the only known Petén records. Should be looked for on Lago Petén-Itzá during migration and winter periods.

Lesser Yellow-headed Vulture   *Cathartes burrovianus*
Visitor outside Tikal

First reported from Petén on 20 March 1978 at Lago Petén-Itzá, and again on 19 March 1980 by C. Leahy. As this vulture is now regularly reported from the Caribbean lowlands (pers. comm. J. Vannini), it might be expected to occur with more frequency in the vast open areas of southern Petén.

Osprey   *Pandion haliaetus*
Rare transient and probable winter resident

Reported flying over Tikal on 18 April 1988 by R. Thorstrom, 14 February 1989 by D. Delaney, and 16 April 1989 by R. Braun, M. Braun, and E. Froelich. Also reported from the Lago Petén-Itzá area in August by C. Leahy and in February by D. Delaney, F. Oatman, and S. Hilty. Known to occur throughout southern Petén.

Gray-headed Kite   *Leptodon cayanensis*
Very rare resident, primarily outside Tikal (no breeding records)

Has been reported in open areas with scattered trees both inside and outside Tikal during the months of February, March, June, September, and December. J. Arvin, F. Oatman, and B. Whitney have observed birds in courtship flights (1988, 1989). Probably a matter of time before breeding records are confirmed. Most frequently reported from roadsides between Santa Elena and the park.

Black-shouldered Kite   *Elanus caeruleus*
Rare resident outside Tikal

Since first reported from Petén at Sayaxché in February 1967 (Eisenmann 1971), this species has dramatically increased in range and relative abundance. First confirmed breeding record from Petén was reported in February 1989 near the Santa Elena airport by J. Arvin, P. Jenny, and F. Oatman. Look for this species in the vast open areas with scattered trees outside Tikal. Also regularly reported at the Santa Elena airport in the open areas along the runway.

Sharp-shinned Hawk   *Accipiter striatus*
Visitor (winter)

Known in Petén only from two records: on 18 February 1977 along road between Lago Petén-Itzá and Sayaxché by F. Oatman, and on 7 February 1988 along the main road at the Tikal entrance by D. Delaney. The white-breasted form, *A. s. chionogaster,* typically from higher elevations, was reported by B. Whitney on 27 February 1988 near Aguada Tikal in the park. The Sharp-shinned Hawk should be looked for in open woodlands, particularly in southwestern Petén during migration periods.

Cooper's Hawk   *Accipiter cooperii*
Hypothetical; possible visitor

A report by P. Jenny on 16 March 1987 along the road between El Remate and Tikal is the only known record from Petén. Should be looked for in open woodlands throughout the department during migration and winter periods.

Black-collared Hawk   *Busarellus nigricollis*
Very rare and localized resident

There are two specimen records from Lago Petén-Itzá (Salvin and Godman 1879–1904; Taibel 1955). D. Delaney reported this species from the lake in February 1988 and 1989. Should be expected throughout the year near the shallow reaches of the lake and in large open bajos, particularly in western Petén.

Solitary Eagle   *Harpyhaliaetus solitarius*
Hypothetical; probable visitor and possible resident

There are three documented reports from Petén, all from
Tikal: a courting pair on 11 March 1986 along the trail to the
tintal forest by F. Oatman and B. Whitney, 18 March 1988 by
E. Cleaveland, and 4 March 1989 by P. Jenny along the road
to Uaxactún. There are also reports of additional sightings in
1990 and 1991 by members of the Peregrine Fund. Although
this species is very difficult to distinguish from the Common
Black-Hawk and Great Black-Hawk, the author believes that
additional documentation will soon confirm this bird's occurrence in Petén and it will be removed from the hypothetical
list.

Short-tailed Hawk   *Buteo brachyurus*
Very rare resident

First reported from Petén and the park when P. Alden reported one flying over Tikal's airstrip on 20 February 1971.
Additional reports of this species (seen flying overhead)
throughout Tikal in January, February, March, June, August,
and November, and annually outside Tikal since 1972. In
1989 R. Thorstrom reported an injured fledgling found on the
road to Uaxactún in the park.

Zone-tailed Hawk   *Buteo albonotatus*
Visitor; possible transient

First reported from Petén and the park flying over the airstrip
on 16 February 1988 by E. Cleaveland. There are other sightings from outside Tikal between El Remate and the park entrance in March and September. Identification of any of the
dark raptors that occur in the region should be approached
with caution. There are several species with dark bodies and

white in the tail (e.g., Snail Kite, Crane Hawk, Common Black-Hawk, Great Black-Hawk, Solitary Eagle, Short-tailed Hawk, Zone-tailed Hawk, and Black Hawk-Eagle).

Crested Eagle   *Morphnus guianensis*
Very rare resident

Reported from east-central Petén in April 1966 and in southeastern Petén in February 1978 (Ellis and Whaley 1981) and January 1974 by C. Leahy. Records from the park include sightings in February through June and in September. P. Jenny and R. Thorstrom reported several very close observations in 1989 and 1990 after luring this species to tape recordings in the forest at Tikal. The very similar Harpy Eagle (*Harpia harpyja*) has not been reported from Petén but should be looked for in the more remote areas of far western portions of the department.

Black-and-white Hawk-Eagle   *Spizastur melanoleucus*
Very rare resident

Reported from Petén near Ceibal on 30 March 1976 by R. A. Rowlett, and near Lago Petén-Itzá in August 1976 by C. Leahy and on 6 March 1988 by P. Jenny and E. Cleaveland. Reported from Tikal in February 1989 by F. Oatman and February 1990 by S. N. G. Howell et al. Typically found in dense lowland forest, which is well represented at Tikal.

Gray-breasted Crake   *Laterallus exilis*
Hypothetical; possible visitor

Reported at Aguada Tikal on 20 October 1991 by L. Prairie and three other observers. Both the Gray-breasted Crake and the allied Black Rail have been reported from Belize (Land 1970).

Spotted Rail   *Pardirallus maculatus*
Hypothetical; possible visitor or localized resident

On 27 February 1991 D. Stejskal reported hearing this species respond to a tape of its call at a large flooded bajo along the road to Uaxactún. This very rare and secretive species has not previously been reported from Guatemala, but suitable habitat for this rail exists throughout Petén.

Common Moorhen   *Gallinula chloropus*
Fairly common transient and winter resident; possible rare and localized resident

First reported from the park at Aguada Tikal between 30 December 1970 and 2 January 1971 by R. Askins. This species has since been reported practically every year from the larger aguadas and Lago Petén-Itzá from August through the end of May. Should be looked for during the summer period, as a resident population may exist on Lago Petén-Itzá.

American Coot   *Fulica americana*
Rare winter resident and probable transient

One specimen record is known from Petén at Lago Petén-Itzá in April 1892 by O. Salvin (British Mus. records). More recent records from this lake include several sightings in January, February, and November from 1975 to 1989 (pers. comm. D. Delaney, F. Oatman, R. A. Rowlett). The only park record was reported at Aguada Tikal on 18 February 1989 by J. Arvin and F. Oatman.

@ Collared Plover   *Charadrius collaris*
Rare resident in southern Petén

First reported from Petén on the road to Poptún seven miles north of the Petén-Izabal border (pair apparently nesting) on 16 June 1988 by S. N. G. Howell. Land (1970) listed this species as an uncommon resident in the Caribbean and Pacific lowlands.

Snowy Plover   *Charadrius alexandrinus*
Visitor

Previously known in Guatemala only from the Pacific lowlands (Dickerman 1975). A sighting on 1 April 1991 near the visitors' center at Tikal by S. N. G. Howell and R. A. Behrstock represents the only known Petén record. As with many other species of shorebirds, this plover could be expected anywhere during the winter and migration periods.

American Avocet   *Recurvirostra americana*
Visitor (winter)

Two Petén records include sightings of single individuals at Lago Petén-Itzá by F. Oatman on 18 and 19 November 1977 (probably of the same bird) and 9 February 1978. Previously known in Guatemala only from the Pacific lowlands (A.O.U. 1983; Land 1970).

Greater Yellowlegs   *Tringa melanoleuca*
Very rare transient (no fall records) and possible winter resident

Reported from the small temporary aguada along the road to Uaxactún in Tikal on 16 February 1988 by E. Cleaveland and on 6 May 1988 by R. Thorstrom. Previously known in Petén only from the southern regions in March and April (Land 1970). Should also be expected during the fall migration period.

Lesser Yellowlegs   *Tringa flavipes*
Very rare transient and possible winter resident

Known in central Petén from a 20 September 1923 specimen

at La Libertad (Van Tyne 1935) and from sight records in February 1978 at Lago Petén-Itzá by F. Oatman and in February 1988 at a small aguada along the road to Uaxactún in Tikal by E. Cleaveland. Also there is a report of this species being found as a prey item in the nest of *Falco deiroleucus* at Tikal (Burnham, Jenny, and Turley 1989).

Western Sandpiper   *Calidris mauri*
Visitor

Known in Petén from one sight record at Tikal on 12 October 1990 by R. Beavers et al. The bird appeared fatigued and was observed from fifteen feet for ten minutes near a rain pool on the airstrip. Distinguishing this species from the closely related Semipalmated Sandpiper (*C. pusilla*) in the adult nonbreeding plumage rests with bill structure (lengths overlap) and call. Primarily a coastal transient in Guatemala but could be found anywhere during migration periods. Most numerous of the wintering small sandpipers in Guatemala (Land 1970).

Least Sandpiper   *Calidris minutilla*
Very rare transient and probable winter resident

Known in Petén from three sight records. F. Oatman reported this species at Lago Petén-Itzá on 9 February 1978, and the first park record was reported on 30 October 1984 by S. N. G. Howell on the airstrip. A second park record was reported on 3 May 1988 by R. Thorstrom. Additional spring and fall records should be expected in appropriate habitats.

Stilt Sandpiper   *Calidris himantopus*
Visitor

A 20 March 1978 sighting at Lago Petén-Itzá by C. Leahy is the only record of this species from Petén. Known elsewhere in Guatemala only from the volcanic lakes (Land 1970). Although not expected, this sandpiper could occur again during migration.

Wilson's Phalarope   *Phalaropus tricolor*
Visitor

A 3 May 1988 sighting at the small temporary aguada along the road to Uaxactún in Tikal by R. Thorstrom is the only known record for Petén. Should be looked for in all aquatic habitats during migration. Previously known in Guatemala only from the Pacific coast (Salvin and Godman 1879–1904).

Laughing Gull   *Larus atricilla*
Visitor (winter) on Lago Petén-Itzá

The first Petén record was reported from Lago Petén-Itzá on 16 January 1970 by P. Alden. There are additional sightings from the lake in January, February, and March (pers. comm. D. Delaney, S. N. G. Howell, J. Lyons, F. Oatman, R. A. Rowlett, J. Tveten; pers. obs. R. Beavers). Most often reported over the water near El Remate on the east side of the lake.

Ring-billed Gull   *Larus delawarensis*
Visitor

The only known records of this species from Petén are two sightings from Lago Petén-Itzá on 9 February 1978 by F. Oatman and 13 March 1988 by C. Aiken and R. Beavers. Known elsewhere in Guatemala only from the volcanic highland lakes (Land 1970).

Royal Tern   *Sterna maxima*
Visitor (winter) on Lago Petén-Itzá

So far reported in Petén only from Lago Petén-Itzá in January 1990 by J. Lyons and in February 1988 and 1989 by D. Delaney. Known elsewhere in Guatemala from the Pacific and

Caribbean coasts (Salvin and Godman 1879–1904) and Lago de Izabal in the Caribbean lowland (pers. comm. C. Leahy).

Rock Dove   *Columba livia*
Very rare and localized resident in towns and villages

Even though Land (1970) indicated this species is domesticated in "most parts of the country," no Tikal records were known until F. Oatman reported three or four birds on 19 and 20 February 1977 near the lodge area. Additional sightings at the park were reported on 15 November 1977 by F. Oatman and on 14 March 1988 by C. Aiken and R. Beavers. This dove is now occasionally seen in the major villages and towns outside Tikal. Probably expanding its range and increasing in abundance both inside and outside the park.

Pale-vented Pigeon   *Columba cayennensis*
Rare resident, primarily outside Tikal

First Petén record was reported by Van Tyne (1935) near Lago Petén-Itzá, where a specimen was taken on 5 August 1923. Also, Taibel (1955) collected a live specimen from the lake area in 1932. Recent records include several sightings in rather open second-growth areas near Flores in February 1978 by F. Oatman, along the road to La Libertad in February 1988 and 1989 by D. Delaney, and along the road between El Remate and Tikal in March 1990 by R. Beavers et al. Park records include sightings on 20 February 1975 by T. Davis, 5 May 1988 by E. Cleaveland, and 15 February 1989 by F. Oatman near the lodge area.

Red-billed Pigeon   *Columba flavirostris*
Very rare resident, primarily outside Tikal

There are numerous sightings of this dove outside Tikal, including records from Sayaxché on 3 February 1969 by N.

Chesterfield, B. Massie, and F. Oatman; from Flores on
18 November 1977 by F. Oatman; from Polol in June 1980
(Brodkin and Brodkin 1981); and along various roads south
and east of Lago Petén-Itzá in February 1988 and 1989 by D.
Delaney and February 1990 by S. N. G. Howell. These birds
were reported from rather open second-growth forested regions and open areas with scattered trees. The only known
park record was reported by J. Arvin and F. Oatman on 14
February 1989 along the Tikal airstrip.

Mourning Dove   *Zenaida macroura*
Very rare transient and winter resident

The first Petén record was reported on 17 November 1977 at
Flores by F. Oatman. The only park record was reported on
28 October 1984 along the Tikal airstrip by S. N. G. Howell.
There are additional sightings from outside the park in the
scrubby, rather open areas along the road between Santa
Elena and the park in February 1988 and 1989 by D. Delaney. Known elsewhere in Guatemala from the arid interior,
western highlands, and Pacific subtropics and lowlands.

Inca Dove   *Columbina inca*
Visitor ?

This species was first reported from Petén by Moore (1859),
but no specific locality was noted. Land (1970) suggested this
species may occur as a resident in the savannas south and west
of Lago Petén-Itzá, supporting a sighting of this species near
the lake on 18 February 1975 by F. Oatman. This dove was
reported from Tikal in March 1972 by T. Davis (pers. comm.
C. Leahy) and on 27–28 November 1976 by R. A. Rowlett.
This species is known to occur in the arid interior and Caribbean lowlands of Guatemala (Land 1970) and should be regularly expected in at least the southern regions of Petén.

Common Ground-Dove   *Columbina passerina*
Hypothetical; possible visitor

First reported from Petén at Tikal on 17 March 1965 by M.
Hundley (special note in Smithe 1966). More recently reported at Tikal along the airstrip on 30 December 1970–
2 January 1971 by R. Askins and on 26 August 1977 by J.
Smith. This dove should be looked for in open brushy areas,
particularly in southern Petén.

Plain-breasted Ground-Dove   *Columbina minuta*
Rare resident outside Tikal

Taibel (1955) collected a specimen from the Lago Petén-Itzá
area on 22 July 1932. There are numerous recent sight records
from this area south to Santa Ana in February 1988 and 1989
by D. Delaney and September 1989 and March 1990 by R.
Beavers et al. This species seems to prefer the disturbed regions outside the park, particularly in the agricultural areas
(milpas).

White-tipped Dove   *Leptotila verreauxi*
Rare resident outside Tikal; visitor at Tikal

Early reports of this species from Petén include specimen records on 14 April and 4 June 1923 from the Lago Petén-Itzá region (Van Tyne 1935) and a live specimen collected in 1932
near Yaxhá by Taibel (1955). Park sightings were reported on
21 February and 15–16 November 1977 by F. Oatman, 10–
11 November 1978 near the old museum by R. A. Rowlett,
and 6 January 1989 along the trail behind the Jaguar Inn by
J. Lyons. There have been sightings south of Lago Petén-Itzá
throughout the year. Seems to prefer dense understory, particularly near second-growth forest edges. Care should be
taken in distinguishing all *Leptotila* species in the field.

Gray-chested Dove   *Leptotila cassini*
Hypothetical; possible very rare resident

Land (1970) indicated this species is a rare resident in Petén. To date, there are no known specimen records from the department, and only one sight record has been reported from Tikal—near the Jaguar Inn on 9 April 1988 by E. Cleaveland. Should be looked for in the ever-increasing dense second-growth forest south of Lago Petén-Itzá and east toward Belize. There are specimen records (Russell 1964) and sight records (pers. comm. R. A. Behrstock, F. Oatman) from extreme western Belize.

Yellow-lored Parrot   *Amazona xantholora*
Hypothetical; possible rare and localized resident in northeastern Petén

A sight record on 4 January 1989 of a pair of Amazons identified as this species was reported by B. Fritz and B. Fenner in the tall forest near Temple III at Tikal. This species is endemic to the Yucatán Peninsula, ranging south to central Belize with specimen records from Chorro and Duck Run near the Petén border (Paynter 1955; Russell 1964). In the drier deciduous forests of the northern Yucatán Peninsula, *A. xantholora* is apparently more common than the similar *A. albifrons.* To the south in Petén, approaching the heavier rain forest, *A. xantholora* is replaced by *A. albifrons* but should be looked for in the extreme northern and eastern portions of the department. Care should be taken in distinguishing these two species.

Black-billed Cuckoo   *Coccyzus erythropthalmus*
Visitor

Sightings on 19 August 1976 in Tikal by C. Leahy and 2 June

1985 near Lago Petén-Itzá by Wendelken and Martin (1986) are the only known records of this species from Petén. Both of these sightings were reported from second-growth forest and forest edge. The June record is somewhat late for this rare migrant species.

Yellow-billed Cuckoo   *Coccyzus americanus*
Visitor

Sightings on 14 August 1978 along the Tikal airstrip by C. Leahy and on 15 April 1989 by R. and M. Braun and E. Froelich along the forest edge at Complex Q in Tikal and a 13 June 1980 report by Brodkin and Brodkin (1981) near the ruins of Polol are the only records from Petén. To be looked for anywhere in the department during migration.

Striped Cuckoo   *Tapera naevia*
Uncommon resident, south of Lago Petén-Itzá

Although there are no specimen records from Petén, this species is probably resident from the Lago Petén-Itzá region south into its previously known range described by Land (1970), where it is more common. There are sight records along various roads on the south side of the lake from February 1988 and 1989 by D. Delaney and June 1988 by S. N. G. Howell. This species seems to prefer the dense brushy undergrowth adjacent to open areas, where it probably parasitizes the nest of the Rufous-breasted Spinetail. No park records are known.

Spectacled Owl   *Pulsatrix perspicillata*
Very rare resident

Known in Petén from Tikal east to the Belize border and south into the Caribbean lowlands (Van Tyne 1935; Land 1970). Records from Tikal include sightings on 17 January

1977 by L. Kilham, on 27 January 1977 by T. Sullivan (pers. comm. C. Leahy), and on 1 March 1990 (heard only) by F. Oatman and D. Stejskal. All three records were reported from the forest adjacent to the airstrip. As long as suitable habitat is available, it is probably just a matter of time before nesting is confirmed at Tikal.

Least Pygmy-Owl   *Glaucidium minutissimum*
Hypothetical; probable rare and localized resident

R. A. Rowlett reported hearing this owl on 12 November 1978 near the North Acropolis at Tikal. F. Oatman and B. Whitney reported two individuals calling near Temple IV at Tikal on 12 March 1986. Depite search efforts, these birds were never seen, but the 1986 birds were tape-recorded. Land (1970) indicates this species "probably" occurs in Petén. To be looked for in forest undergrowth and forest edge throughout the region.

Ferruginous Pygmy-Owl   *Glaucidium brasilianum*
Rare resident

Reported regularly outside Tikal from the Lago Petén-Itzá area by D. Delaney, east to Belize (photograph by R. A. Behrstock), and south to Sayaxché by F. Oatman. F. Oatman also reported this species along the Tikal airstrip on 16 February 1975 and 11 March 1986 (tape-recorded). Previously known in Tikal only from bone remains found in burial caches (see Smithe 1966). The continued practice of clearing the forest in Petén may be enhancing the spread of this species.

Lesser Nighthawk   *Chordeiles acutipennis*
Rare transient and possible winter resident; possible localized resident in open savannas south of Lago Petén-Itzá, more common during migration

Land (1970) indicated this species is found over much of the country during migration and may be a resident in parts of Guatemala. There are several records of this species from Petén, including sightings on 30 March 1976 near Ceibal by R. A. Rowlett, on 31 January–13 February 1988 and 1989 by D. Delaney, and on 11 October 1990 by R. Beavers along the road between Santa Elena and the park. D. Delaney's report included flocks of up to fifteen individuals. A suspected Lesser Nighthawk was reported over the Tikal airstrip in September 1977 by R. Askins, and R. A. Behrstock and S. N. G. Howell reported two individuals flying over the Main Plaza on 30 March 1991.

White-collared Swift   *Streptoprocne zonaris*
Very rare visitor (winter)

Reported on several occasions from Tikal between 15 November and 28 March by D. Delaney, C. Leahy, and F. Oatman. More common in southern Petén during this period when *S. zonaris* typically moves out of the central highlands to lower elevations (Land 1970).

Chimney Swift   *Chaetura pelagica*
Visitor; probable rare transient

A sighting on 1 April 1991 of several migrating flocks at Tikal by R. A. Behrstock and S. N. G. Howell is the only known record from Petén. The observers reported the differentiating characteristics from the Vaux's Swift, which is similar (and simultaneously was seen nearby). Although a definite locality is unknown, one previous record (specimen) was reported from Guatemala by Salvin and Godman (1879–1904). Could occur anywhere in Petén during migration. Care should be taken in distinguishing the two *Chaetura* swifts.

Black-crested Coquette   *Lophornis helenae*
Visitor

Known in Petén from six sight records, all at Tikal. Reported
along the trail near Temple I on 18 January 1977 by C.
Leahy, along the trail to the tintal forest on 11, 15 February
1978 and 26 March 1981 by R. A. Rowlett, and in the escobal
forest along the road to Uaxactún on 26 February 1984 and
27 February 1985 (photographed) by Wendelken and Martin
(1986). This species may prove to be a resident in southern
Petén and a regular winter visitor to the park.

Azure-crowned Hummingbird   *Amazilia cyanocephala*
Visitor

First reported from Petén in the southeastern region near
Poptún in March 1862 by O. Salvin (British Mus. records).
The only other record is a well-documented sighting at Tikal
on 15 April 1989 by R. Braun and E. Froelich. The bird was
found along the trail between Group G and Temple VI (Temple of Inscriptions) near a brushy second-growth clearing.
Might be expected again, particularly during the nonbreeding
season.

Berylline Hummingbird   *Amazilia beryllina*
Hypothetical; possible visitor

Sightings have been reported from southern Petén on 24 August 1977 by J. Smith, from Tikal on 28 August 1977 by J.
Smith, and in the open woods of Lost World at Tikal on 18
January 1989 by B. Mealy, J. Powell, and three other observers. The January bird was well documented, noting all characteristics to distinguish it from similar *A. tzacatl* and *A. yuca-
tanensis*. This species is known to wander to lower, more
humid forests during the nonbreeding season (Monroe 1968;
A.O.U. 1983).

Ruby-throated Hummingbird   *Archilochus colubris*
Rare transient and winter resident

First Petén record was reported by O. Salvin near Santa Ana
in April 1862 (British Mus. records). First reported from Tikal
in the lodge area on 17 January 1977 (and several times
through 28 January) by C. Leahy. There have since been several sight records in the park from September through the end
of March. Most records have come from brushy edges next to
open areas, particularly near the lodges and other dwellings in
the park.

Rufous-breasted Spinetail   *Synallaxis erythrothorax*
Uncommon and localized resident south of Lago Petén-Itzá

First reported from Petén near Sayaxché on 16 March 1967 by
P. Alden, and at Tikal along the airstrip on 2 February 1975
by C. Leahy. This species is now presumed to be resident in
the dense second-growth forests and thickets along the roads
from Lago Petén-Itzá south, as there are numerous recent
sight records throughout the year (including a tape recording).
Land (1970) noted that this species is probably fairly common
in southern Petén.

Wedge-billed Woodcreeper   *Glyphoryncus spirurus*
Very rare resident

First reported in Petén by Ridgway (1901–50) from the southern reaches of the department. Reported from Tikal on 19 February 1971 by P. Alden, 4 February 1975 by C. Leahy, 13–19
February 1978 by R. Askins, 25 February 1984 by Wendelken
and Martin (1986), and 20 September 1989 by R. Beavers et
al. All of these records occurred along the forest edge, where
there was dense understory nearby. Sightings outside the park
were reported on 3 February 1969 at Ceibal by F. Oatman
and on 13–14 February 1989 along the road to Poptún by D.

Delaney. This bird should be looked for at lower levels of the denser tall and second-growth forests and forest edge throughout the region.

Great Antshrike   *Taraba major*
Very rare and localized resident ?

The only records from Petén were sightings reported by D. Delaney on 12 February 1989 approximately ten kilometers east of Santa Elena and on 18 February 1989 approximately eight kilometers southeast of Santa Elena. R. A. Rowlett reported hearing this species along the airstrip at Tikal in March 1976. All of these records were reported from dense second growth. Previously known in Petén only from "sources of the Rio de la Pasión," presumably in the extreme southwestern part of the department (Ridgway 1901–50). Should be found localized in suitable dense habitat from Lago Petén-Itzá south into its previously known range.

Yellow-bellied Elaenia   *Elaenia flavogaster*
Rare resident outside Tikal

There are specimen records noted throughout the open areas of the central Petén by Salvin and Godman (1879–1904), Van Tyne (1935), and Taibel (1955). First park record was reported by E. P. Edwards near the lodge on 7 June 1957 (pers. comm. K. Ladwig), and a second record by F. Oatman on 16 November 1977. D. Delaney reported this species on several occasions in February 1988 and 1989 along various roads south of Lago Petén-Itzá to La Libertad. Seems to prefer rather open areas adjacent to thick secondary growth.

Slate-headed Tody-Flycatcher   *Todirostrum sylvia*
Uncommon resident; more numerous in southern Petén

First reported from Petén on 21 April 1923 at San Miguel,

northwest of Lago Petén-Itzá (Van Tyne 1935). There are numerous sight records from disturbed areas both inside and outside Tikal in January, February, March, June, and December. The thickets and forest edge along the Tikal airstrip is the best available habitat in the park for this species.

Common Tody-Flycatcher   *Todirostrum cinereum*
Very rare and localized resident

Specimen records were noted by Van Tyne (1935) and Taibel (1955) from the Lago Petén-Itzá area, northwest to Chuntuquí, and south to La Libertad. Two relatively recent sightings from Lago Petén-Itzá include a report by F. Oatman on 18 February 1975 and one by J. Smith on 31 August 1977. This Tody-Flycatcher typically prefers second-growth brush. No park records are known.

Acadian Flycatcher   *Empidonax virescens*
Hypothetical; possible visitor or transient

Reported only once from Petén at Tikal in March 1981 by R. A. Rowlett (reportedly identified by call note and field marks). Land (1970) notes that this flycatcher should pass through Guatemala regularly during migration periods. Typically found in woodland and woodland edge.

Willow Flycatcher   *Empidonax traillii*
Uncommon transient (no confirmed spring records)

Smithe (1966) describes the Alder Flycatcher (*E. alnorum*) as the common fall migrant *Empidonax* at Tikal. After further examination by A. R. Phillips of fifteen specimens collected by F. B. Smithe, six were determined to be *E. alnorum* and nine to be *E. traillii* (pers. comm. R. A. Paynter, Jr.). Despite the abundance of this bird in Tikal during fall migration, there are no confirmed spring records. Perhaps there is a much broader or more coastal migratory route in the spring. As with all *Empidonax* species, field identification is nearly impossible unless birds are vocalizing.

Vermilion Flycatcher   *Pyrocephalus rubinus*
Rare resident outside Tikal

This species occurs throughout the year in the cleared areas south of Tikal and the open savannas south and southwest of Lago Petén-Itzá. Several specimen records were reported from central Petén by Moore (1859), Van Tyne (1935), and Taibel (1955). Numerous sight records were reported along the road to La Libertad in June 1980 by Brodkin and Brodkin (1981) and in February 1988 by D. Delaney and S. Hilty, and south to Ceibal by R. A. Rowlett in March 1976. Also reported near Lago Petén-Itzá in February 1975, 1977, and November 1977 by F. Oatman, March 1976 and November 1978 by R. A. Rowlett, January 1989 by J. Sparrow, and February 1988 by D. Delaney.

Couch's Kingbird   *Tyrannus couchii*
Fairly common resident

Since the separation of this species from *T. melancholius* (Traylor 1979), both have been regularly reported from open areas inside and outside Tikal. These two species can be found side-by-side along the Tikal airstrip. Although the two can sometimes be found in equal numbers (particularly in February and March), during the period from 1986 to 1990 *T. couchii* appeared overall to be more common than *T. melancholicus*. These species should be distinguished in the field only by vocalization. (Tropical emits a rapid trill or twittering "pip-pip-pip-pip," and Couch's a "kip" or "pik" and "ch-weer" or a rolling "breeeer.")

Fork-tailed Flycatcher   *Tyrannus savana*
Uncommon resident, more numerous in southern Petén

There are specimen records from central Petén on 27 June
1923 (Van Tyne 1935) and 11 July 1932 (Taibel 1955). Sight
records were reported near Ceibal in March 1976 by R. A.
Rowlett; near La Libertad in June 1980 by Brodkin and Brodkin (1981); along the road between Flores and Poptún (twenty
individuals) in October 1984 by S. N. G. Howell; near the
Flores–Santa Elena area in February 1975, November 1977,
and February 1978 by F. Oatman; in February 1988 by D.
Delaney and S. Hilty; in June 1988 by S. N. G. Howell; and
in September 1989 by C. Aiken et al. There is one report
from Tikal in April 1965 (special note in Smithe 1966). This
species should be looked for in open areas with scattered trees,
from which they are often seen perched atop and sallying up-
ward to catch flying insects.

Lovely Cotinga   *Cotinga amabilis*
Visitor; probable very rare and localized resident

There are several sight records from Tikal on 15 January 1970
by P. Alden, on 18 March 1988 and in July 1990 by R. Thorstrom (male photographed), and on 23 June 1988 and 10 February 1991 by S. N. G. Howell. Most sightings in the park
were reported from high in the canopy near the Main Plaza
and north and south of the central park region. Records outside Tikal include sightings along the road between La Libertad and Sayaxché on 6 December 1975 by R. Ridgely (pers.
comm. C. Leahy), at Cerro Cahuí on the north side of Lago
Petén-Itzá on 20 March 1987 by P. Jenny and E. Cleaveland,
and along the road to Poptún on 17 February 1989 by D. Delaney. Although seasonal movements are thought to occur in
this species, the wide geographic and temporal distribution of

these records suggests the Lovely Cotinga is a localized resident in Petén.

Tree Swallow   *Tachycineta bicolor*
Very rare transient and probable winter resident

Land (1970) indicated this species is found over "much of the country" but gives no records for Petén. Sight records were reported at Tikal on 5 February 1969, 7 February 1978, and 25, 28 February 1990 by F. Oatman, and 26 August 1977 by J. Smith; and in the Flores–Santa Elena area on 9 February 1978 by F. Oatman and 19 March 1990 by R. Beavers. Look for this species in all open areas during the migration periods.

Bank Swallow   *Riparia riparia*
Very rare transient

Sighted over the aguadas in Tikal on 26 August 1977 by J. Smith and on 5 May 1988 by R. Thorstrom. This transient species is probably more common in riparian habitats found in western and southern Petén.

Cliff Swallow   *Hirundo pyrrhonota*
Visitor ?; possible very rare transient (no fall records)

Land (1970) stated this species is likely to be seen anywhere in Guatemala but does not indicate any records from Petén. Sight records were reported from Tikal flying over the aguada near the airstrip on 18 April 1972 by T. Davis (pers. comm. C. Leahy) and on 21 March 1990 by R. Beavers and J. Tveten. Should also be expected during the fall migration period.

Band-backed Wren   *Campylorhynchus zonatus*
Very rare resident

This wren has been reported from a variety of habitats and localities in Petén. There are specimen records from Gavilán in eastern Petén on 1 July 1923 (Van Tyne 1935). Sight records were reported along the road between La Libertad and Sayaxché on 17 March 1967 by M. Bowes and P. Alden, near Ceibal on 3 February 1969 by F. Oatman and on 30 March 1976 by R. A. Rowlett, at Polol on 13 June 1980 by Brodkin and Brodkin (1981), and in a riparian woodland near the Belize border on 13 February 1987 by F. Oatman and R. A. Rowlett. The first park record was reported on 24 March 1990 near the Jungle Lodge by C. Bookout, J. McMillon, and B. Noel.

House Wren (Southern)   *Troglodytes aedon*
Uncommon resident

There are specimen records from Flores on 9 April 1931, Plancha de Piedra (near Belize) on 2 July 1931, La Libertad on 8 November 1923 (Van Tyne 1935), and near Lago Petén-Itzá on 7 June 1932 (Taibel 1955). Since the first park record was reported on 26 August 1986 by C. Aiken, there have been numerous sightings from both inside and outside Tikal. This species has been reported from dense thickets along forest edges and adjacent to clearings.

@ **Nightingale Wren**   *Microcerculus philomela*
Very rare resident in southern Petén

Land (1970) indicated this wren is known in Guatemala from the humid forest undergrowth of the Caribbean lowland and "probably" southern Petén. A specimen was reported from the forest between Cahabón (Alta Verapaz) and San Luis (Petén) by Salvin and Godman (1879–1904). J. Smith reported several singing Nightingale Wrens on 23 August 1977 in a "relatively undisturbed forest" adjacent to the road between San Luis and Poptún in southeastern Petén, and S. N. G. Howell reported a singing bird along the same road approximately fifteen miles north of the Petén-Izabal border on 16 June 1988.

Blue-gray Gnatcatcher   *Polioptila caerulea*
Uncommon transient and winter resident

Specimens have been reported by Van Tyne (1935) from Remate
on 30 July 1923 and La Libertad between 3 September and
9 November 1923 (questioned by Phillips 1986–91, pt. 2).
There are numerous recent sight records from both inside and
outside the park from July through May. A resident form endemic to the Yucatán Peninsula (*deppei*) may occur in the
northern reaches of Petén (Land 1970). This race differs from
the nominate wintering form (*caerulea*) by its slightly smaller
size.

Black Catbird   *Melanoptila glabrirostris*
Very rare and localized resident, possibly only a visitor
(seasonal?)

There are specimen records from Ixtinto in eastern Petén on
27 June 1923 (Van Tyne 1935) and near Lago Petén-Itzá on
19 June 1932 (Taibel 1955). Two sight records include a report on 26 August 1986 in a brushy open area near the trail to
Temple VI (Temple of Inscriptions) by C. Aiken (first park
record) and on 18 March 1990 by R. Beavers and J. Tveten
along the brushy roadside near the Santa Elena airport. To be
looked for in any brushy open areas in northern Petén south
to the Santa Elena–Flores region, probably the southern limit
of its range.

Tropical Mockingbird   *Mimus gilvus*
Very rare resident in extreme eastern and southwestern Petén

Land (1970) reported this mockingbird from southwestern Petén. Reported in extreme eastern Petén, near the Belize border,
on 1 April 1989 by D. Stejskal and B. Whitney. To be looked
for in scrubby second-growth areas outside central Petén.

Solitary Vireo   *Vireo solitarius*
Very rare transient and probable winter resident

Known in Petén only from several sight records. There are reports from Tikal on 17 March 1965 (special note in Smithe 1966), 27 January 1977 by C. Leahy, 26 August 1977 by J. Smith, 7–8 February 1978 by F. Oatman, 13 March 1988 by C. Aiken, 26 February 1990 by F. Oatman and D. Stejskal, and 8 October 1990 by R. Beavers, C. Bookout, and C. Sloan. There is one report from Ceibal on 23 February 1969 by F. Oatman.

Warbling Vireo   *Vireo gilvus*
Very rare transient

Since the first Petén record was reported from Tikal on 17 February 1975 by F. Oatman, subsequent reports from the park were noted in February, April, and November (pers. comm. R. Braun, F. Oatman, R. A. Rowlett). Most birds were observed in the open forest and forest edge.

Rufous-browed Peppershrike   *Cyclarhis gujanensis*
Uncommon resident outside Tikal, locally south of Lago Petén-Itzá

Since the first Petén sight record on 14 August 1976 near Lago Petén-Itzá by C. Leahy, this species has been found on numerous occasions south of the lake by R. Beavers, D. Delaney, and F. Oatman. Most records have come from second-growth forest edges adjacent to open areas south of Lago Petén-Itzá. S. N. G. Howell reported this species as common between Poptún and the southern Petén border.

Golden-winged Warbler   *Vermivora chrysoptera*
Rare transient and probable winter resident

First reported in literature from Petén at Tikal on 25 February 1984 by Wendelken and Martin (1986). There have been additional reports from the forest and forest edge in the park practically every year in the spring, 6 February through 18 April (pers. comm. R. Braun, D. Delaney, C. Leahy, F. Oatman), and in the fall on 27 October 1984 by S. N. G. Howell, and 8, 11 October 1990 by R. Beavers, C. Bookout, and C. Sloan.

Orange-crowned Warbler   *Vermivora celata*
Visitor

An uncommon winter visitor to the highlands, Caribbean lowlands, and southern Petén (Land 1970). A park record was noted near the lodges on 9 October 1990 by R. Beavers, C. Bookout, and C. Sloan. Could be found anywhere in Petén during the winter and migratory periods.

Nashville Warbler   *Vermivora ruficapilla*
Very rare transient and winter resident

Known in Petén from three winter sight records along the forest edge at Tikal: 21 February 1975 and 2 January 1976 by C. Leahy and 19 January 1989 by B. Mealy. Reported as a fairly common winter visitor in the highlands of Guatemala (Land 1970).

Virginia's Warbler   *Vermivora virginiae*
Hypothetical; possible visitor

There is one detailed report of this species on 23 February 1977 from the shrubs next to Lago Petén-Itzá by F. Oatman. This very unusual record was well documented, noting all characteristics to distinguish it from similar species. However, a report of this species from the 1988 Belize Christmas Bird Count has been questioned based on the difficulty (or impossibility) of separating *V. virginiae* from some pale individuals of *V. ruficapilla* (see Howell 1989). Additional documentation (probably from a specimen) is needed to confirm occurrence south and east of the Isthmus of Tehuantepec.

Northern Parula   *Parula americana*
Very rare visitor (winter)

Sight records of this species have been reported from the forest edge at Tikal in January 1970, January and February 1971, and March 1967 (pers. comm. P. Alden, R. Askins). Previously known in Guatemala only from the Pacific and Caribbean lowlands (Land 1970). Should be looked for throughout the park during the winter and migration periods.

Tropical Parula   *Parula pitiayumi*
Visitor

Known in Petén only from three park sight records: on 10–12 April 1965 (special note in Smithe 1966), on 8 February 1978 by F. Oatman, and in March 1981 by R. A. Rowlett. To be looked for in open woodland and forest edge anywhere in Petén.

Cape May Warbler   *Dendroica tigrina*
Very rare visitor (winter)

First reported from Petén on 2 February 1975 at the lodge area in Tikal by C. Leahy. There are additional sightings from the same area by C. Leahy on 4 and 20 February 1975 (possibly of same bird). Regularly reported elsewhere in Guatemala from the highlands and Caribbean lowlands (Mason 1976; pers. comm. C. Leahy).

* Yellow-rumped Warbler (Aud.)   *Dendroica c. auduboni*
Hypothetical; possible visitor

T. Davis reported an apparent straggler of this race in Tikal

on 17–18 April 1972 (pers. comm. C. Leahy), the only record
from Petén. A fairly common winter visitor and resident in
the highlands of Guatemala (Land 1970).

Yellow-throated Warbler   *Dendroica dominica*
Very rare transient and winter resident

Reported from Tikal in March 1972 and February 1973 by C.
Leahy, February 1975 by T. Davis (pers. comm. C. Leahy)
and F. Oatman, November 1977 by F. Oatman, March 1988
by C. Aiken and R. Beavers, January 1989 by J. Lyons, and
February and March 1990 by F. Oatman, R. Beavers, C.
Bookout, and C. Sloan. Most observations have been from the
open woodlands near the lodges.

@ Grace's Warbler   *Dendroica graciae*
Hypothetical; possible visitor (resident?) in southern Petén

Known in Petén only from one report by J. Smith on 5 September 1977 in a grove of pines approximately forty kilometers south of Flores. Known elsewhere in Guatemala from the
pine and pine-oak woodlands of the Caribbean subtropics
(Land 1970). To be looked for in the pine ridges of southeastern Petén.

Bay-breasted Warbler   *Dendroica castanea*
Very rare transient

Reported from Tikal on 18 April 1972 by T. Davis (pers.
comm. C. Leahy), in March 1981 by R. A. Rowlett, on 7 May
1982 by Wendelken and Martin (1986), on 27 October 1984
by S. N. G. Howell, on 26 February 1990 by F. Oatman, and
on 2 March 1990 (possibly same bird) by D. Stejskal (last two
records are exceptionally early dates). Most sightings came
from the forest edge in the central portions of the park. Land
(1970) reported this species only from Alta Verapaz.

Swainson's Warbler   *Limnothlypis swainsonii*
Visitor

Known in Petén only from a series of sight records at Tikal on
8 February 1978 by F. Oatman (probably the first record for
Guatemala), and 16, 17, 18 February 1989 (possibly same
bird) by F. Oatman and J. Arvin. These birds were well documented, noting differentiating field marks from the fairly common Worm-eating Warbler. Recently reported from extreme
southern Chiapas, Mexico (Rangel-Salazar and Vega-Rivera
1989).

Gray-crowned Yellowthroat   *Geothlypis poliocephala*
Rare and localized resident, primarily outside Tikal

There are numerous sight records of this species from various
areas around Lago Petén-Itzá and Sayaxché (pers. comm. C.
Leahy, F. Oatman) and specimen records from Chuntuquí on
8–11 May 1923 and Gavilán on 1 July 1923 (Van Tyne 1935).
This warbler was recorded from Tikal along the airstrip on
5 February 1969 by F. Oatman and N. Chesterfield and 10–
11 February 1987 by F. Oatman and R. A. Rowlett. Normally
found in brushy fields and grassy areas.

Canada Warbler   *Wilsonia canadensis*
Very rare transient

There are five records of this species from Petén, all from the
forest and forest edge in the central park region. Reported on
7 March 1972 by N. Proctor; 27 November 1976 by R. A.
Rowlett (exceptionally early and late dates); 20 September
1989 by R. Braun and M. Braun; two individuals on 23 September 1989 by C. Aiken, R. Beavers, and C. Bookout; and
11 October 1990 by R. Beavers, C. Bookout, and C. Sloan.
Known throughout much of the remainder of Guatemala as
an uncommon transient (Land 1970).

Rufous-capped Warbler   *Basileuterus rufifrons*
Hypothetical; possible visitor (winter)

Reported in Petén on 24 August 1977 along the road near
Santa Ana by J. Smith, 16 January 1989 along the road between Santa Elena and the park by J. Sparrow, and 18 January
1989 near Temple IV in Tikal by C. Aiken. Even though this
species is known to range down into the Caribbean subtropics
near the southern Petén border, additional documentation is
needed to confirm its occurrence in Petén. It is interesting to
note the two January sight records were reported within two
days of one another, with neither observer having knowledge
of the other's report. This species is typically found in brushy
woodlands, open second-growth forest, and forest edge.

Blue-hooded Euphonia   *Euphonia elegantissima*
Hypothetical; possible visitor

This species was reported on 28 February 1988 along the trail
near Complex Q in Tikal by J. Moore (pers. comm. F. Oatman). This species is known to range down into the Caribbean lowlands and subtropics, but its occurrence in Petén remains unconfirmed without additional documentation. This
euphonia may be found along forest edges and open second-
growth forest and is known to wander to lowlands after breeding season (Isler and Isler 1987).

Blue-gray Tanager   *Thraupis episcopus*
Uncommon resident

A tanager of the open woodlands, open second-growth forest
and forest edge, more common outside Tikal. There are numerous records from outside the park, including two specimen records from Flores and La Libertad on 3 October 1923
(Van Tyne 1935) and another specimen, probably from the

Lago Petén-Itzá area in 1856 (Moore 1859). Numerous sightings from Tikal have been reported between December and March by R. Askins, C. Aiken, R. Beavers, and F. Oatman. Mostly seen in the park in rather open woodland near the lodges.

Hepatic Tanager   *Piranga flava*
Visitor

A specimen record from Poptún in March 1862 by O. Salvin (British Mus. records) and a sight record from approximately two miles south of Santa Elena along the road to Poptún on 22 March 1990 by R. Beavers and J. Tveten are the only records of this tanager from Petén. A lowland resident form (*figlina*) is known to occur in the pine ridge savannas of southeastern Petén (Isler and Isler 1987).

Scarlet Tanager   *Piranga olivacea*
Very rare transient

Known from scattered localities throughout Petén in March, April, and October (Land 1970, pers. obs. R. Beavers). There is one very unusual late fall sight record reported from Tikal on 4 December 1975 (pers. comm. C. Leahy). Could be found in any number of habitats during migration.

Crimson-collared Tanager   *Ramphocelus sanguinolentus*
Rare and localized resident south of Lago Petén-Itzá

There is one specimen record from an undetermined locality in Petén (probably near Lago Petén-Itzá) reported by Moore (1859); however, Land (1970) indicates this species ranges only into the southern portions of the department. There are numerous sight records from second-growth thickets and brushy areas just south of Lago Petén-Itzá in February and March by R. Beavers and D. Delaney, from near Sayaxché in February by F. Oatman, and from extreme southern Petén in September by J. Smith.

@ **Scarlet-rumped Tanager**   *Ramphocelus passerinii*
Rare resident in southern Petén

Known in Petén only from the humid forest edge and second-growth forest in the southern portion of the department (Land 1970). J. Smith reported several individuals of this species while passing through this region in August and September 1977. More common in the Caribbean lowlands to the south.

Grayish Saltator   *Saltator coerulescens*
Uncommon resident, primarily outside Tikal

This saltator is a resident in the second-growth forest and forest edge outside Tikal, as confirmed by specimen records reported by Van Tyne (1935) and Taibel (1955). Reports from various areas in the park include sightings in January by J. Sparrow, February by F. Oatman, March by R. A. Rowlett, April (special note in Smithe 1966), November by R. A. Rowlett, and December by R. Askins. To be expected anywhere in Petén where second-growth habitat is found.

Buff-throated Saltator   *Saltator maximus*
Rare resident south of Lago Petén-Itzá; visitor at Tikal

This saltator was first reported from Petén at Tikal in March 1976 and November 1978 by R. A. Rowlett and at Lago Petén-Itzá in February 1978 by F. Oatman. This species has most often been reported from second-growth thickets and forest edge along various roads from Lago Petén-Itzá south.

Olive Sparrow   *Arremonops rufivirgatus*
Rare and localized resident south of Lago Petén-Itzá

Known only from the open second-growth brushy areas south

of Lago Petén-Itzá and from the savannas near La Libertad and Santa Ana. There have been sight records from these areas in February 1988 and 1989 by D. Delaney and June 1980 by Brodkin and Brodkin (1981), and a specimen record from April 1956 (Smithe 1966). These records are presumably of the endemic Yucatán race (*verticalis*).

Yellow-faced Grassquit   *Tiaris olivacea*
Rare resident outside Tikal

Known in Petén from several specimen records east and south of Lago Petén-Itzá in June and September to November 1923 (Van Tyne 1935) and from an undetermined date in 1856 (Moore 1859). There are several sight records from February, March, June, September, and November by R. Beavers, D. Delaney, S. N. G. Howell, F. Oatman, and R. A. Rowlett from open brushy areas and abandoned milpas along the roads outside the park, south to Poptún.

Botteri's Sparrow   *Aimophila botterii*
Rare resident outside Tikal

The endemic race of this species (*petenica*) is found in the taller grassy fields and brush areas from the Lago Petén-Itzá area south and southwest into the open savannas. Specimen records have been noted by Salvin (1863) and Van Tyne (1935). Sight records have been reported near Polol in June 1980 (Brodkin and Brodkin 1981), near Flores in February 1978 by F. Oatman, and south of Lago Petén-Itzá in February 1988 by D. Delaney.

@ Rusty Sparrow   *Aimophila rufescens*
Rare resident in southern Petén

There is a specimen record from the Poptún area dated March 1862 (British Mus. record) and sight records from the same region on 5 September 1977 by J. Smith and 16 June 1988 by S. N. G. Howell. To be looked for throughout southern Petén in brushy growth in pine woodlands, second-growth forests, and savannas.

Red-winged Blackbird   *Agelaius phoeniceus*
Rare and localized resident near Lago Petén-Itzá

Specimen records were reported from near Lago Petén-Itzá in April, June, and July by Moore (1859), Van Tyne (1935), and Taibel (1955). Sightings were reported from the lake area in February 1975, 1977, and 1978 by F. Oatman; August 1977 by J. Smith; January 1989 by B. Mealy; and February 1989 by D. Delaney. To be looked for in the grassy edges and marshes of Lago Petén-Itzá.

Eastern Meadowlark   *Sturnella magna*
Uncommon and localized resident outside Tikal

Specimen records were reported from Poptún by Sclater (1886) and from La Libertad by Van Tyne (1935). Brodkin and Brodkin (1981) reported this species from the savannas between La Libertad and Polol in June 1980, and F. Oatman reported a small group from Lago Petén-Itzá on 10–11 February 1978. To be looked for throughout the grassy savannas south and southwest of Lago Petén-Itzá.

Bronzed Cowbird   *Molothrus aeneus*
Uncommon resident, primarily outside Tikal

Specimen records were reported from Flores in April through June 1923 by Van Tyne (1935). There are sight records from cleared agricultural sites near El Remate and Santa Elena, and along the roads south of Lago Petén-Itzá in February 1969 and 1978 by F. Oatman and February 1988 and 1989 by D. Delaney. There are two sight records from Tikal on 17 March

1965 by M. Hundley (special note in Smithe 1966) and 24 March 1981 by R. A. Rowlett. D. Delaney contends this species is often overlooked and goes undetected in central Petén.

Altamira Oriole   *Icterus gularis*
Visitor

Known in Petén from one sight record on 9 February 1992 by R. A. Behrstock and S. N. G. Howell. This bird was reported singing near Aguada Dimmick along the airstrip and was heard again on 11 February 1992. The Altamira Oriole is a fairly common resident in the arid interior and on the Pacific slopes of Guatemala (Land 1970).

Yellow-billed Cacique   *Amblycercus holosericeus*
Rare resident outside Tikal

Specimen records have been reported from the Lago Petén-Itzá area by Moore (1859) and by Taibel (1955). There are several sight records from dense brushy areas adjacent to second-growth forests outside Tikal near La Libertad (Brodkin and Brodkin 1981), at Ceibal and Sayaxché by F. Oatman, and along various roads around Lago Petén-Itzá by R. Beavers, D. Delaney et al., and F. Oatman. An unusual sighting of eight caciques in the East Plaza at Tikal was reported on 15 April 1989 by R. Braun, M. Braun, and E. Froelich.

Appendix 1: List of Petén Species by Status

T = Reported from Tikal National Park

Residents

Great Tinamou	*Tinamus major*	
Little Tinamou	*Crypturellus soui*	
Thicket Tinamou	*Crypturellus cinnamomeus*	T
Slaty-breasted Tinamou	*Crypturellus boucardi*	T
Least Grebe	*Tachybaptus dominicus*	T
Neotropic Cormorant	*Phalacrocorax brasilianus*	T
Anhinga	*Anhinga anhinga*	T
Bare-throated Tiger-Heron	*Tigrisoma mexicanum*	T
Little Blue Heron	*Egretta caerulea*	T
Cattle Egret	*Bubulcus ibis*	T

Residents

Common Name	Scientific Name	Status
@.. Chestnut-bellied Heron	*Agamia agami*	T
Boat-billed Heron	*Cochlearius cochlearius*	
@ Black-bellied Whistling-Duck	*Dendrocygna autumnalis*	
Muscovy Duck	*Cairina moschata*	T
Black Vulture	*Coragyps atratus*	T
Turkey Vulture	*Cathartes aura*	T
King Vulture	*Sarcoramphus papa*	T
Gray-headed Kite	*Leptodon cayanensis*	
Hook-billed Kite	*Chondrohierax uncinatus*	
Black-shouldered Kite	*Elanus caeruleus*	T
Snail Kite	*Rostrhamus sociabilis*	T
Double-toothed Kite	*Harpagus bidentatus*	T
Bicolored Hawk	*Accipiter bicolor*	T
Crane Hawk	*Geranospiza caerulescens*	T
White Hawk	*Leucopternis albicollis*	
Great Black-Hawk	*Buteogallus urubitinga*	
Black-collared Hawk	*Busarellus nigricollis*	
Gray Hawk	*Buteo nitidus*	T
Roadside Hawk	*Buteo magnirostris*	T
Short-tailed Hawk	*Buteo brachyurus*	T

Residents

Crested Eagle	*Morphnus guianensis*	T
Black-and-white Hawk-Eagle	*Spizastur melanoleucus*	T
Black Hawk-Eagle	*Spizaetus tyrannus*	T
Ornate Hawk-Eagle	*Spizaetus ornatus*	T
Laughing Falcon	*Herpetotheres cachinnans*	T
Barred Forest-Falcon	*Micrastur ruficollis*	T
Collared Forest-Falcon	*Micrastur semitorquatus*	T
Bat Falcon	*Falco rufigularis*	T
Orange-breasted Falcon	*Falco deiroleucus*	T
Plain Chachalaca	*Ortalis vetula*	T
Crested Guan	*Penelope purpurascens*	T
Great Curassow	*Crax rubra*	T
Ocellated Turkey	*Agriocharis ocellata*	T
Spotted Wood-Quail	*Odontophorus guttatus*	T
Singing Quail	*Dactylortyx thoracicus*	
Black-throated Bobwhite	*Colinus nigrogularis*	
Ruddy Crake	*Laterallus ruber*	
Gray-necked Wood-Rail	*Aramides cajanea*	T
Purple Gallinule	*Porphyrula martinica*	T
Sungrebe	*Heliornis fulica*	T

Residents

Common Name	Scientific Name	Status
Limpkin	*Aramus guarauna*	T
@ Collared Plover	*Charadrius collaris*	T
Northern Jacana	*Jacana spinosa*	T
Rock Dove	*Columba livia*	T
Pale-vented Pigeon	*Columba cayennensis*	T
Scaled Pigeon	*Columba speciosa*	T
Red-billed Pigeon	*Columba flavirostris*	T
Short-billed Pigeon	*Columba nigrirostris*	T
Plain-breasted Ground-Dove	*Columbina minuta*	
Ruddy Ground-Dove	*Columbina talpacoti*	T
Blue Ground-Dove	*Claravis pretiosa*	T
White-tipped Dove	*Leptotila verreauxi*	T
Gray-fronted Dove	*Leptotila rufaxilla*	T
Ruddy Quail-Dove	*Geotrygon montana*	T
Olive-throated Parakeet	*Aratinga nana*	T
Brown-hooded Parrot	*Pionopsitta haemototis*	T
White-crowned Parrot	*Pionus senilis*	T
White-fronted Parrot	*Amazona albifrons*	T
Red-lored Parrot	*Amazona autumnalis*	T
Mealy Parrot	*Amazona farinosa*	T

Residents

Squirrel Cuckoo	*Piaya cayana*	T
Striped Cuckoo	*Tapera naevia*	T
Pheasant Cuckoo	*Dromococcyx phasianellus*	T
Groove-billed Ani	*Crotophaga sulcirostris*	T
Vermiculated Screech-Owl	*Otus guatemalae*	T
Spectacled Owl	*Pulsatrix perspicillata*	T
Ferruginous Pygmy-Owl	*Glaucidium brasilianum*	T
Mottled Owl	*Ciccaba virgata*	T
Black-and-white Owl	*Ciccaba nigrolineata*	T
Pauraque	*Nyctidromus albicollis*	
Yucatan Poorwill	*Nyctiphrynus yucatanicus*	
@.. Great Potoo	*Nyctibius grandis*	T
Common Potoo	*Nyctibius griseus*	T
Vaux's Swift	*Chaetura vauxi*	T
Lesser Swallow-tailed Swift	*Panyptila cayennensis*	T
Long-tailed Hermit	*Phaethornis superciliosus*	T
Little Hermit	*Phaethornis longuemareus*	T
Scaly-breasted Hummingbird	*Phaeochroa cuvierii*	
Wedge-tailed Sabrewing	*Campylopterus curvipennis*	T
White-necked Jacobin	*Florisuga mellivora*	T

Residents

Green-breasted Mango	*Anthracothorax prevostii*	T
Fork-tailed Emerald	*Chlorostilbon canivetii*	T
White-bellied Emerald	*Amazilia candida*	T
Rufous-tailed Hummingbird	*Amazilia tzacatl*	T
Buff-bellied Hummingbird	*Amazilia yucatanensis*	T
Purple-crowned Fairy	*Heliothryx barroti*	T
Black-headed Trogon	*Trogon melanocephalus*	T
Violaceous Trogon	*Trogon violaceus*	T
Collared Trogon	*Trogon collaris*	T
Slaty-tailed Trogon	*Trogon massena*	T
Tody Motmot	*Hylomanes momotula*	T
Blue-crowned Motmot	*Momotus momota*	T
Ringed Kingfisher	*Ceryle torquata*	T
Amazon Kingfisher	*Chloroceryle amazona*	T
Green Kingfisher	*Chloroceryle americana*	T
American Pygmy Kingfisher	*Chloroceryle aenea*	T
White-necked Puffbird	*Bucco macrorhynchos*	T
White-whiskered Puffbird	*Malacoptila panamensis*	T
Rufous-tailed Jacamar	*Galbula ruficauda*	T
Emerald Toucanet	*Aulacorhynchus prasinus*	T

Residents

Collared Aracari	T	*Pteroglossus torquatus*
Keel-billed Toucan	T	*Ramphastos sulfuratus*
Black-cheeked Woodpecker	T	*Melanerpes pucherani*
Golden-fronted Woodpecker	T	*Melanerpes aurifrons*
Smoky-brown Woodpecker	T	*Veniliornis fumigatus*
Golden-olive Woodpecker	T	*Piculus rubiginosus*
Chestnut-colored Woodpecker	T	*Celeus castaneus*
Lineated Woodpecker	T	*Dryocopus lineatus*
Pale-billed Woodpecker	T	*Campephilus guatemalensis*
Rufous-breasted Spinetail	T	*Synallaxis erythrothorax*
Buff-throated Foliage-gleaner	T	*Automolus ochrolaemus*
Plain Xenops	T	*Xenops minutus*
Scaly-throated Leaftosser	T	*Sclerurus guatemalensis*
Tawny-winged Woodcreeper	T	*Dendrocincla anabatina*
Ruddy Woodcreeper	T	*Dendrocincla homochroa*
Olivaceous Woodcreeper	T	*Sittasomus griseicapillus*
Wedge-billed Woodcreeper	T	*Glyphorynchus spirurus*
Strong-billed Woodcreeper	T	*Xiphocolaptes promeropirhynchus*
Barred Woodcreeper	T	*Dendrocolaptes certhia*
Ivory-billed Woodcreeper	T	*Xiphorhynchus flavigaster*

Residents

Streak-headed Woodcreeper	*Lepidocolaptes souleyetii*	T
Great Antshrike	*Taraba major*	T
Barred Antshrike	*Thamnophilus doliatus*	T
Russet Antshrike	*Thamnistes anabatinus*	T
Plain Antvireo	*Dysithamnus mentalis*	T
Dot-winged Antwren	*Microrhopias quixensis*	T
Dusky Antbird	*Cercomacra tyrannina*	T
Black-faced Antthrush	*Formicarius analis*	T
Paltry Tyrannulet	*Zimmerius vilissimus*	T
Yellow-bellied Tyrannulet	*Ornithion semiflavum*	T
Northern Beardless-Tyrannulet	*Camptostoma imberbe*	T
Greenish Elaenia	*Myiopagis viridicata*	T
Yellow-bellied Elaenia	*Elaenia flavogaster*	T
Ochre-bellied Flycatcher	*Mionectes oleagineus*	T
Sepia-capped Flycatcher	*Leptopogon amaurocephalus*	T
Northern Bentbill	*Oncostoma cinereigulare*	T
Slate-headed Tody-Flycatcher	*Todirostrum sylvia*	T
Common Tody-Flycatcher	*Todirostrum cinereum*	T
Eye-ringed Flatbill	*Rhynchocyclus brevirostris*	T
Yellow-olive Flycatcher	*Tolmomyias sulphurescens*	T

Residents

Common Name	Scientific Name	
Stub-tailed Spadebill	*Platyrinchus cancrominus*	T
Royal Flycatcher	*Onychorhynchus coronatus*	T
Ruddy-tailed Flycatcher	*Terenotriccus erythrurus*	T
Sulphur-rumped Flycatcher	*Myiobius sulphureipygius*	T
Tropical Pewee	*Contopus cinereus*	T
@ . . Black Phoebe	*Sayornis nigricans*	
Vermilion Flycatcher	*Pyrocephalus rubinus*	
Bright-rumped Attila	*Attila spadiceus*	T
Rufous Mourner	*Rhytipterna holerythra*	T
Yucatan Flycatcher	*Myiarchus yucatanensis*	T
Dusky-capped Flycatcher	*Myiarchus tuberculifer*	T
Brown-crested Flycatcher	*Myiarchus tyrannulus*	T
Great Kiskadee	*Pitangus sulphuratus*	T
Boat-billed Flycatcher	*Megarynchus pitangua*	T
Social Flycatcher	*Myiozetetes similis*	T
Tropical Kingbird	*Tyrannus melancholicus*	T
Couch's Kingbird	*Tyrannus couchii*	T
Fork-tailed Flycatcher	*Tyrannus savana*	T
Cinnamon Beard	*Pachyramphus cinnamomeus*	T
Gray-collared Becard	*Pachyramphus major*	T

T T T T T T T T T T T T T T T T T T T T

Residents

Common Name	Scientific Name
Rose-throated Becard	*Pachyramphus aglaiae*
Masked Tityra	*Tityra semifasciata*
Black-crowned Tityra	*Tityra inquisitor*
Rufous Piha	*Lipaugus unirufus*
Thrush-like Manakin	*Schiffornis turdinus*
White-collared Manakin	*Manacus candei*
Red-capped Manakin	*Pipra mentalis*
Gray-breasted Martin	*Progne chalybea*
Mangrove Swallow	*Tachycineta albilinea*
Northern Rough-winged Swallow	*Stelgidopteryx seripennis*
Green Jay	*Cyanocorax yncas*
Brown Jay	*Cyanocorax morio*
Yucatan Jay	*Cyanocorax yucatanicus*
Band-backed Wren	*Campylorhynchus zonatus*
Spot-breasted Wren	*Thryothorus maculipectus*
Carolina Wren (White-browed)	*Thryothorus ludovicianus*
House Wren (Southern)	*Troglodytes aedon*
White-bellied Wren	*Uropsila leucogastra*
White-breasted Wood-Wren	*Henicorhina leucosticta*
@ Nightingale Wren	*Microcerculus philomela*

Residents

Common name	Scientific name	
Long-billed Gnatwren	*Ramphocaenus melanurus*	T
Tropical Gnatcatcher	*Polioptila plumbea*	T
Clay-colored Robin	*Turdus grayi*	T
White-throated Robin	*Turdus assimilis*	T
Black Catbird	*Melanoptila glabrirostris*	T
Tropical Mockingbird	*Mimus gilvus*	
Mangrove Vireo	*Vireo pallens*	
Tawny-crowned Greenlet	*Hylophilus ochraceiceps*	T
Lesser Greenlet	*Hylophilus decurtatus*	T
Green Shrike-Vireo	*Vireolanius pulchellus*	T
Rufous-browed Peppershrike	*Cyclarhis gujanensis*	T
Gray-crowned Yellowthroat	*Geothlypis poliocephala*	
Golden-crowned Warbler	*Basileuterus culicivorus*	T
Gray-throated Chat	*Granatellus sallaei*	T
Bananaquit	*Coereba flaveola*	T
Golden-masked Tanager	*Tangara larvata*	T
Green Honeycreeper	*Chlorophanes spiza*	T
Red-legged Honeycreeper	*Cyanerpes cyaneus*	T
Scrub Euphonia	*Euphonia affinis*	T
Yellow-throated Euphonia	*Euphonia hirundinacea*	T

Residents

Common Name	Scientific Name	Status
Olive-backed Euphonia	*Euphonia gouldi*	T
Blue-gray Tanager	*Thraupis episcopus*	T
Yellow-winged Tanager	*Thraupis abbas*	T
Gray-headed Tanager	*Eucometis penicillata*	T
Black-throated Shrike-Tanager	*Lanio aurantius*	T
Red-crowned Ant-Tanager	*Habia rubica*	T
Red-throated Ant-Tanager	*Habia fuscicauda*	T
Rose-throated Tanager	*Piranga roseogularis*	T
White-winged Tanager	*Piranga leucoptera*	T
Crimson-collared Tanager	*Ramphocelus sanguinolentus*	
@ Scarlet-rumped Tanager	*Ramphocelus passerinii*	T
Grayish Saltator	*Saltator coerulescens*	T
Buff-throated Saltator	*Saltator maximus*	T
Black-headed Saltator	*Saltator atriceps*	T
Black-faced Grosbeak	*Caryothraustes poliogaster*	T
Northern Cardinal	*Cardinalis cardinalis*	T
Blue-black Grosbeak	*Cyanocompsa cyanoides*	T
Blue Bunting	*Cyanocompsa parellina*	T
Orange-billed Sparrow	*Arremon aurantiirostris*	T
Olive Sparrow	*Arremonops rufivirgatus*	T

Residents

Common name	Scientific name	
Green-backed Sparrow	*Arremonops chloronotus*	T
Blue-black Grassquit	*Volatinia jacarina*	T
White-collared Seedeater	*Sporophila torqueola*	T
Thick-billed Seed-Finch	*Oryzoborus funereus*	T
Yellow-faced Grassquit	*Tiaris olivacea*	
Botteri's Sparrow	*Aimophila botterii*	
@ Rusty Sparrow	*Aimophila rufescens*	
@ Chipping Sparrow	*Spizella passerina*	
Red-winged Blackbird	*Agelaius phoeniceus*	T
Eastern Meadowlark	*Sturnella magna*	T
Melodious Blackbird	*Dives dives*	T
Great-tailed Grackle	*Quiscalus mexicanus*	T
Bronzed Cowbird	*Molothrus aeneus*	T
Giant Cowbird	*Scaphidura oryzivora*	T?
Black-cowled Oriole	*Icterus dominicensis*	T
Yellow-backed Oriole	*Icterus chrysater*	T
Yellow-tailed Oriole	*Icterus mesomelas*	
Yellow-billed Cacique	*Amblycercus holosericeus*	
@.. Chestnut-headed Oropendola	*Psarocolius wagleri*	T
Montezuma Oropendola	*Psarocolius montezuma*	

Summer Residents

		Status
American Swallow-tailed Kite	*Elanoides forficatus*	T
Plumbeous Kite	*Ictinia plumbea*	T
Streaked Flycatcher	*Myiodynastes maculatus*	T
Sulphur-bellied Flycatcher	*Myiodynastes luteiventris*	T
Piratic Flycatcher	*Legatus leucophaius*	T
Yellow-green Vireo	*Vireo flavoviridis*	T

Transients and Winter Residents

(* known only as transients, not overwintering)

		Status
Pied-billed Grebe	*Podilymbus podiceps*	T
Great Blue Heron	*Ardea herodias*	T
Great Egret	*Casmerodius albus*	T
Snowy Egret	*Egretta thula*	T
Tricolored Heron	*Egretta tricolor*	
Green-backed Heron	*Butorides striatus*	T
Yellow-crowned Night-Heron	*Nyctanassa violacea*	T
Blue-winged Teal	*Anas dicors*	T
Osprey	*Pandion haliaetus*	T
Broad-winged Hawk*	*Buteo platypterus*	T
American Kestrel	*Falco sparverius*	T

Transients and Winter Residents

Sora	*Porzana carolina*	T
Common Moorhen	*Gallinula chloropus*	T
American Coot	*Fulica americana*	T
Killdeer	*Charadrius vociferus*	T
Black-necked Stilt	*Himantopus mexicanus*	T
Greater Yellowlegs	*Tringa melanoleuca*	T
Lesser Yellowlegs	*Tringa flavipes*	T
Solitary Sandpiper	*Tringa solitaria*	T
Spotted Sandpiper	*Actitis macularia*	T
Least Sandpiper	*Calidris minutilla*	T
Pectoral Sandpiper★	*Calidris melanotos*	T
Common Snipe	*Gallinago gallinago*	T
Mourning Dove	*Zenaida macroura*	T
Lesser Nighthawk	*Chordeiles acutipennis*	T
Common Nighthawk★	*Chordeiles minor*	T
Ruby-throated Hummingbird	*Archilochus colubris*	T
Belted Kingfisher	*Ceryle alcyon*	T
Olive-sided Flycatcher	*Contopus borealis*	T
Eastern Wood-Pewee	*Contopus virens*	T
Yellow-bellied Flycatcher	*Empidonax flaviventris*	T

Transients and Winter Residents

Common Name	Scientific Name	
Alder Flycatcher*	*Empidonax alnorum*	T
Willow Flycatcher*	*Empidonax traillii*	T
Least Flycatcher	*Empidonax minimus*	T
Great Crested Flycatcher	*Myiarchus crinitus*	T
Eastern Kingbird*	*Tyrannus tyrannus*	T
Scissor-tailed Flycatcher	*Tyrannus forficatus*	T
Purple Martin*	*Progne subis*	T
Tree Swallow	*Tachycineta bicolor*	T
Bank Swallow*	*Riparia riparia*	T
Barn Swallow*	*Hirundo rustica*	T
Blue-gray Gnatcatcher	*Polioptila caerulea*	T
Veery*	*Catharus fuscescens*	T
Gray-cheeked Thrush*	*Catharus minimus*	T
Swainson's Thrush*	*Catharus ustulatus*	T
Wood Thrush	*Hylocichla mustelina*	T
Gray Catbird	*Dumetella carolinensis*	T
Cedar Waxwing	*Bombycilla cedrorum*	T
White-eyed Vireo	*Vireo griseus*	T
Solitary Vireo	*Vireo solitarius*	T
Yellow-throated Vireo	*Vireo flavifrons*	T

Transients and Winter Residents

Common Name	Scientific Name	T
Warbling Vireo*	*Vireo gilvus*	T
Philadelphia Vireo	*Vireo philadelphicus*	T
Red-eyed Vireo	*Vireo olivaceus*	T
Blue-winged Warbler	*Vermivora pinus*	T
Golden-winged Warbler	*Vermivora chrysoptera*	T
Tennessee Warbler	*Vermivora peregrina*	T
Nashville Warbler	*Vermivora ruficapilla*	T
Yellow Warbler	*Dendroica petechia*	T
Chestnut-sided Warbler	*Dendroica pensylvanica*	T
Magnolia Warbler	*Dendroica magnolia*	T
Yellow-rumped Warbler (Myrtle)	*Dendroica coronata*	T
Black-throated Green Warbler	*Dendroica virens*	T
Blackburnian Warbler*	*Dendroica fusca*	T
Yellow-throated Warbler	*Dendroica dominica*	T
Bay-breasted Warbler*	*Dendroica castanea*	T
Black-and-white Warbler	*Mniotilta varia*	T
American Redstart	*Setophaga ruticilla*	T
Prothonotary Warbler	*Protonotaria citrea*	T
Worm-eating Warbler	*Helmitheros vermivorus*	T
Ovenbird	*Seiurus aurocapillus*	T

Transients and Winter Residents

Common Name	Scientific Name	Status
Northern Waterthrush	*Seiurus noveboracensis*	T
Louisiana Waterthrush	*Seiurus motacilla*	T
Kentucky Warbler	*Oporornis formosus*	T
Common Yellowthroat	*Geothlypis trichas*	T
Hooded Warbler	*Wilsonia citrina*	T
Wilson's Warbler	*Wilsonia pusilla*	T
Canada Warbler★	*Wilsonia canadensis*	T
Yellow-breasted Chat	*Icteria virens*	T
Summer Tanager	*Piranga rubra*	T
Scarlet Tanager★	*Piranga olivacea*	T
Rose-breasted Grosbeak	*Pheucticus ludovicianus*	T
Blue Grosbeak	*Guiraca caerulea*	T
Indigo Bunting	*Passerina cyanea*	T
Painted Bunting	*Passerina ciris*	T
Dickcissel★	*Spiza americana*	T
Orchard Oriole	*Icterus spurius*	T
Northern Oriole	*Icterus galbula*	T

Visitors

Common Name	Scientific Name	Status
Brown Pelican	*Pelecanus occidentalis*	T

Visitors

Common Name	Scientific Name	
Pinnated Bittern	*Botaurus pinnatus*	
.. American Bittern	*Botaurus lentiginosus*	
Least Bittern	*Ixobrychus exilis*	T
. Reddish Egret	*Egretta rufescens*	T
Black-crowned Night-Heron	*Nycticorax nycticorax*	T
White Ibis	*Eudocimus albus*	
Jabiru	*Jabiru mycteria*	T
Wood Stork	*Mycteria americana*	T
Northern Shoveler	*Anas clypeata*	T
Ring-necked Duck	*Aythya collaris*	
.. Lesser Yellow-headed Vulture	*Cathartes burrovianus*	
Sharp-shinned Hawk	*Accipiter striatus*	T
Common Black-Hawk	*Buteogallus anthracinus*	T
Zone-tailed Hawk	*Buteo albonotatus*	T
Snowy Plover	*Charadrius alexandrinus*	T
.. Semipalmated Plover	*Charadrius semipalmatus*	
American Avocet	*Recurvirostra americana*	
.. Upland Sandpiper	*Bartramia longicauda*	
Western Sandpiper	*Calidris mauri*	T
. White-rumped Sandpiper	*Calidris fuscicollis*	T

Visitors

Common name	Scientific name	Status
Stilt Sandpiper	*Calidris himantopus*	
Wilson's Phalarope	*Phalaropus tricolor*	T
Laughing Gull	*Larus atricilla*	
Ring-billed Gull	*Larus delawarensis*	
Royal Tern	*Sterna maxima*	T
Inca Dove	*Columbina inca*	T
Scarlet Macaw	*Ara macao*	T
Black-billed Cuckoo	*Coccyzus erythropthalmus*	T
Yellow-billed Cuckoo	*Coccyzus americanus*	T
.. Barn Owl	*Tyto alba*	T
. Chuck-will's-widow	*Caprimulgus carolinensis*	T
White-collared Swift	*Streptoprocne zonaris*	
Chimney Swift	*Chaetura pelagica*	
Black-crested Coquette	*Lophornis helenae*	
Azure-crowned Hummingbird	*Amazilia cyanocephala*	
@.. Stripe-tailed Hummingbird	*Eupherusa eximia*	
.. Long-billed Starthroat	*Heliomaster longirostris*	
. Keel-billed Motmot	*Electron carinatum*	T (possible resident)
.. Acorn Woodpecker	*Melanerpes formicivorus*	
Yellow-bellied Sapsucker	*Sphyrapicus varius*	T

Visitorss

Common name	Scientific name	
Greater Pewee	*Contopus pertinax*	T
.. White-throated Flycatcher	*Empidonax albigularis*	
Lovely Cotinga	*Cotinga amabilis*	T
.. Sinaloa Martin	*Progne sinaloae*	
Cliff Swallow	*Hirundo pyrrhonota*	T
.. Gray-breasted Wood-Wren	*Henicorhina leucophrys*	
Orange-crowned Warbler	*Vermivora celata*	T
Northern Parula	*Parula americana*	T
Tropical Parula	*Parula pitiayumi*	T
Cape May Warbler	*Dendroica tigrina*	T
. Cerulean Warbler	*Dendroica cerulea*	T
Swainson's Warbler	*Limnothlypis swainsonii*	T
. Mourning Warbler	*Oporornis philadelphia*	
Hepatic Tanager	*Piranga flava*	
.. Western Tanager	*Piranga ludoviciana*	
.. Flame-colored Tanager	*Piranga bidentata*	(possible resident)
. Grasshopper Sparrow	*Ammodramus savannarum*	
. Bobolink	*Dolichonyx oryzivorus*	T
Altamira Oriole	*Icterus gularis*	T

Appendix 2: List of Petén Species Based on Specimen Records from Petén (with reference footnotes)*

Great Tinamou	*Tinamus major*	8,9,11,12
Little Tinamou	*Crypturellus soui*	8
Thicket Tinamou	*Crypturellus cinnamomeus*	8,9
Slaty-breasted Tinamou	*Crypturellus boucardi*	8,12
Pied-billed Grebe	*Podilymbus podiceps*	1,3
Least Grebe	*Tachybaptus dominicus*	12
Neotropic Cormorant	*Phalacrocorax brasilianus*	1,3,9
Anhinga	*Anhinga anhinga*	1,3,9,11
Bare-throated Tiger-Heron	*Tigrisoma mexicanum*	3,8,11,12
Great Egret	*Casmerodius albus*	9
Little Blue Heron	*Egretta caerulea*	8,12

Common Name	Scientific Name	
Cattle Egret	*Bubulcus ibis*	10
Green-backed Heron	*Butorides striatus*	8,12
@.. Chestnut-bellied Heron	*Agamia agami*	3
Black-crowned Night-Heron	*Nycticorax nycticorax*	1,12
Yellow-crowned Night-Heron	*Nyctanassa violacea*	8,9
Boat-billed Heron	*Cochlearius cochlearius*	1,3
Muscovy Duck	*Cairina moschata*	1,3
King Vulture	*Sarcoramphus papa*	11
Hook-billed Kite	*Chondrohierax uncinatus*	8,12
American Swallow-tailed Kite	*Elanoides forficatus*	8
Snail Kite	*Rostrhamus sociabilis*	1,3,8,9
Double-toothed Kite	*Harpagus bidentatus*	12
Plumbeous Kite	*Ictinia plumbea*	3,8,9,11
Bicolored Hawk	*Accipiter bicolor*	8,12
Crane Hawk	*Geranospiza caerulescens*	11,12
White Hawk	*Leucopternis albicollis*	8,12
Great Black-Hawk	*Buteogallus urubitinga*	8,11
Black-collared Hawk	*Busarellus nigricollis*	3,9
Gray Hawk	*Buteo nitidus*	8,11
Roadside Hawk	*Buteo magnirostris*	3,8,9,12
Broad-winged Hawk	*Buteo platypterus*	12

Crested Eagle	*Morphnus guianensis*	15
Black Hawk-Eagle	*Spizaetus tyrannus*	12
Ornate Hawk-Eagle	*Spizaetus ornatus*	8,9,12
Laughing Falcon	*Herpetotheres cachinnans*	11,12
Barred Forest-Falcon	*Micrastur ruficollis*	12
Collared Forest-Falcon	*Micrastur semitorquatus*	12
American Kestrel	*Falco sparverius*	8
Bat Falcon	*Falco rufigularis*	8,12
Orange-breasted Falcon	*Falco deiroleucus*	12
Plain Chachalaca	*Ortalis vetula*	8,9,11,12
Crested Guan	*Penelope purpurascens*	8,9,11,12
Great Curassow	*Crax rubra*	1,3,8,9,11,12
Ocellated Turkey	*Agriocharis ocellata*	1,5,6,8,9,12
Spotted Wood-Quail	*Odontophorus guttatus*	8,12
Singing Quail	*Dactylortyx thoracicus*	12
Black-throated Bobwhite	*Colinus nigrogularis*	8,9
Ruddy Crake	*Laterallus ruber*	8,12
Gray-necked Wood-Rail	*Aramides cajanea*	8,9,11,12
Purple Gallinule	*Porphyrula martinica*	1,3,8,9
American Coot	*Fulica americana*	3
Sungrebe	*Heliornis fulica*	12

Limpkin	*Aramus guarauna*	8,9
.. Semipalmated Plover	*Charadrius semipalmatus*	8
Killdeer	*Charadrius vociferus*	12
Black-necked Stilt	*Himantopus mexicanus*	11,12
Northern Jacana	*Jacana spinosa*	1,3,8,9,11
Lesser Yellowlegs	*Tringa flavipes*	8
Solitary Sandpiper	*Tringa solitaria*	8,12
Spotted Sandpiper	*Actitis macularia*	8,12
.. Upland Sandpiper	*Bartramia longicauda*	3
. White-rumped Sandpiper	*Calidris fuscicollis*	12
Pectoral Sandpiper	*Calidris melanotos*	12
Pale-vented Pigeon	*Columba cayennensis*	8
Scaled Pigeon	*Columba speciosa*	1,3,8,12
Short-billed Pigeon	*Columba nigrirostris*	8,12
Inca Dove	*Columbina inca*	1,3
Plain-breasted Ground-Dove	*Columbina minuta*	7,9
Ruddy Ground-Dove	*Columbina talpacoti*	1,3,8,12
Blue Ground-Dove	*Claravis pretiosa*	3,8,9,12
White-tipped Dove	*Leptotila verreauxi*	8,9
Gray-fronted Dove	*Leptotila rufaxilla*	8,12
Ruddy Quail-Dove	*Geotrygon montana*	8,12

Scarlet Macaw	*Ara macao*	3,9
Olive-throated Parakeet	*Aratinga nana*	3,8,9,11,12
Brown-hooded Parrot	*Pionopsitta haematotis*	11,12
White-crowned Parrot	*Pionus senilis*	8,9,12
White-fronted Parrot	*Amazona albifrons*	3,8,9,12
Red-lored Parrot	*Amazona autumnalis*	8,9,11,12
Mealy Parrot	*Amazona farinosa*	3,8,9,12
Squirrel Cuckoo	*Piaya cayana*	1,3,8,9,11,12
Pheasant Cuckoo	*Dromococcyx phasianellus*	8,12
Groove-billed Ani	*Crotophaga sulcirostris*	8,11,12
.. Barn Owl	*Tyto alba*	8
Vermiculated Screech-Owl	*Otus guatemalae*	8,12
Spectacled Owl	*Pulsatrix perspicillata*	8
Mottled Owl	*Ciccaba virgata*	8,11,12
Black-and-white Owl	*Ciccaba nigrolineata*	12
Pauraque	*Nyctidromus albicollis*	3,8,9,12
Yucatan Poorwill	*Nyctiphrynus yucatanicus*	8,9,12
. Chuck-will's-widow	*Caprimulgus carolinensis*	12
@ .. Great Potoo	*Nyctibius grandis*	11,13
Common Potoo	*Nyctibius griseus*	8
Vaux's Swift	*Chaetura vauxi*	8

Common Name	Scientific Name	Codes
Long-tailed Hermit	*Phaethornis superciliosus*	3,8,12
Little Hermit	*Phaethornis longuemareus*	8,12
Scaly-breasted Hummingbird	*Phaeochroa cuvierii*	12
Wedge-tailed Sabrewing	*Campylopterus curvipennis*	8,12
White-necked Jacobin	*Florisuga mellivora*	8,12
Green-breasted Mango	*Anthracothorax prevostii*	3,8
Fork-tailed Emerald	*Chlorostilbon canivetii*	8,12
White-bellied Emerald	*Amazilia candida*	8,12
Azure-crowned Hummingbird	*Amazilia cyanocephala*	3
Rufous-tailed Hummingbird	*Amazilia tzacatl*	3,8,9,12
Buff-bellied Hummingbird	*Amazilia yucatanensis*	2,3,12
@ .. Stripe-tailed Hummingbird	*Eupherusa eximia*	3 ?.
Purple-crowned Fairy	*Heliothryx barroti*	3,8,12
Ruby-throated Hummingbird	*Archilochus colubris*	3
.. Long-billed Starthroat	*Heliomaster longirostris*	3
Black-headed Trogon	*Trogon melanocephalus*	8,9,11,12
Violaceous Trogon	*Trogon violaceus*	8,9,12
Collared Trogon	*Trogon collaris*	12
Slaty-tailed Trogon	*Trogon massena*	8,11,12
Tody Motmot	*Hylomanes momotula*	8,12
Blue-crowned Motmot	*Momotus momota*	8,9,12

Common Name	Scientific Name	Records
Ringed Kingfisher	*Ceryle torquata*	1,3,8,9,12
Belted Kingfisher	*Ceryle alcyon*	12
Amazon Kingfisher	*Chloroceryle amazona*	9,12
Green Kingfisher	*Chloroceryle americana*	8,9,11,12
American Pygmy Kingfisher	*Chloroceryle aenea*	3,8,11,12
White-necked Puffbird	*Bucco macrorhynchos*	12
White-whiskered Puffbird	*Malacoptila panamensis*	8,12
Rufous-tailed Jacamar	*Galbula ruficauda*	8,9,11,12
Emerald Toucanet	*Aulacorhynchus prasinus*	8,12
Collared Aracari	*Pteroglossus torquatus*	8,11,12
Keel-billed Toucan	*Ramphastos sulfuratus*	3,8,9,11,12
.. Acorn Woodpecker	*Melanerpes formicivorus*	9
Black-cheeked Woodpecker	*Melanerpes pucherani*	8,12
Golden-fronted Woodpecker	*Melanerpes aurifrons*	8,9,11,12
Yellow-bellied Sapsucker	*Sphyrapicus varius*	12
Smoky-brown Woodpecker	*Veniliornis fumigatus*	8,11,12
Golden-olive Woodpecker	*Piculus rubiginosus*	8,11,12
Chestnut-colored Woodpecker	*Celeus castaneus*	8,9,11
Lineated Woodpecker	*Dryocopus lineatus*	8,12
Pale-billed Woodpecker	*Campephilus guatemalensis*	8,9,11,12
Buff-throated Foliage-gleaner	*Automolus ochrolaemus*	8,12

Plain Xenops	*Xenops minutus*	7,8,12
Scaly-throated Leaftosser	*Sclerurus guatemalensis*	8,12
Tawny-winged Woodcreeper	*Dendrocincla anabatina*	3,8,12
Ruddy Woodcreeper	*Dendrocincla homochroa*	3,8,12
Olivaceous Woodcreeper	*Sittasomus griseicapillus*	8,12
Wedge-billed Woodcreeper	*Glyphorynchus spirurus*	7,9
Strong-billed Woodcreeper	*Xiphocolaptes promeropirhynchus*	3,12
Barred Woodcreeper	*Dendrocolaptes certhia*	12
Ivory-billed Woodcreeper	*Xiphorhynchus flavigaster*	8,12
Streak-headed Woodcreeper	*Lepidocolaptes souleyetii*	3,8
Great Antshrike	*Taraba major*	7
Barred Antshrike	*Thamnophilus doliatus*	8,9,12
Russet Antshrike	*Thamnistes anabatinus*	12
Plain Antvireo	*Dysithamnus mentalis*	7,8,12
Dot-winged Antwren	*Microrhopias quixensis*	7,8,12
Dusky Antbird	*Cercomacra tyrannina*	7,8,12
Black-faced Antthrush	*Formicarius analis*	7,8,11,12
Paltry Tyrannulet	*Zimmerius vilissimus*	13 ?
Yellow-bellied Tyrannulet	*Ornithion semiflavum*	12
Northern Beardless-Tyrannulet	*Camptostoma imberbe*	8,12
Greenish Elaenia	*Myiopagis viridicata*	8,12

Common Name	Scientific Name	Records
Yellow-bellied Elaenia	*Elaenia flavogaster*	3,8,9
Ochre-bellied Flycatcher	*Mionectes oleagineus*	8,12
Sepia-capped Flycatcher	*Leptopogon amaurocephalus*	8,12
Northern Bentbill	*Oncostoma cinereigulare*	12
Slate-headed Tody-Flycatcher	*Todirostrum sylvia*	8
Common Tody-Flycatcher	*Todirostrum cinereum*	8,9
Eye-ringed Flatbill	*Rhynchocyclus brevirostris*	8,12
Yellow-olive Flycatcher	*Tolmomyias sulphurescens*	8,12
Stub-tailed Spadebill	*Platyrinchus cancrominus*	8,12
Royal Flycatcher	*Onychorhynchus coronatus*	8,11,12
Ruddy-tailed Flycatcher	*Terenotriccus erythrurus*	8,12
Sulphur-rumped Flycatcher	*Myiobius sulphureipygius*	3,8,12
Olive-sided Flycatcher	*Contopus borealis*	12
Eastern Wood-Pewee	*Contopus virens*	8,12
Tropical Pewee	*Contopus cinereus*	8,12
Yellow-bellied Flycatcher	*Empidonax flaviventris*	12
Alder Flycatcher	*Empidonax alnorum*	12
Willow Flycatcher	*Empidonax traillii*	12
.. White-throated Flycatcher	*Empidonax albigularis*	8,9
Least Flycatcher	*Empidonax minimus*	8,12
Vermilion Flycatcher	*Pyrocephalus rubinus*	1,3,8,9

Common name	Scientific name	
Bright-rumped Attila	*Attila spadiceus*	8,12
Rufous Mourner	*Rhytipterna holerythra*	12
Yucatan Flycatcher	*Myiarchus yucatanensis*	8,9,12
Dusky-capped Flycatcher	*Myiarchus tuberculifer*	7,8,12
Great Crested Flycatcher	*Myiarchus crinitus*	12
Brown-crested Flycatcher	*Myiarchus tyrannulus*	8,12
Great Kiskadee	*Pitangus sulphuratus*	12
Boat-billed Flycatcher	*Megarynchus pitangua*	8,12
Social Flycatcher	*Myiozetetes similis*	8,9,12
Streaked Flycatcher	*Myiodynastes maculatus*	8,12
Sulphur-bellied Flycatcher	*Myiodynastes luteiventris*	1,3,8,12
Piratic Flycatcher	*Legatus leucophaius*	12
Tropical Kingbird	*Tyrannus melancholicus*	8,9,12
Couch's Kingbird	*Tyrannus couchii*	14
Eastern Kingbird	*Tyrannus tyrannus*	1,12
Scissor-tailed Flycatcher	*Tyrannus forficatus*	12
Fork-tailed Flycatcher	*Tyrannus savana*	3,8,9
Cinnamon Becard	*Pachyramphus cinnamomeus*	8,12
Gray-collared Becard	*Pachyramphus major*	12
Rose-throated Becard	*Pachyramphus aglaiae*	12
Masked Tityra	*Tityra semifasciata*	8,12

Black-crowned Tityra	*Tityra inquisitor*	1,3,9,12
Rufous Piha	*Lipaugus unirufus*	12
Thrush-like Manakin	*Schiffornis turdinus*	8,12
White-collared Manakin	*Manacus candei*	1,3,8,9,12
Red-capped Manakin	*Pipra mentalis*	8,12
.. Sinaloa Martin	*Progne sinaloae*	13?
Gray-breasted Martin	*Progne chalybea*	3,8,9,12
Mangrove Swallow	*Tachycineta albilinea*	3,8
Northern Rough-winged Swallow	*Stelgidopteryx seripennis*	8,12
Barn Swallow	*Hirundo rustica*	12
Green Jay	*Cyanocorax yncas*	8,12
Brown Jay	*Cyanocorax morio*	8,9,11,12
Yucatan Jay	*Cyanocorax yucatanicus*	3,9,12
Band-backed Wren	*Campylorhynchus zonatus*	8
Spot-breasted Wren	*Thryothorus maculipectus*	3,8,12
Carolina Wren (White-browed)	*Thryothorus ludovicianus*	2,3,8,12
House Wren (Southern)	*Troglodytes aedon*	8,9
White-bellied Wren	*Uropsila leucogastra*	8,12
White-breasted Wood-Wren	*Henicorhina leucosticta*	3,8,12
.. Gray-breasted Wood-Wren	*Henicorhina leucophrys*	8
@ Nightingale Wren	*Microcerculus philomela*	3 ?

Common name	Scientific name	Codes
Long-billed Gnatwren	*Ramphocaenus melanurus*	8,12
Blue-gray Gnatcatcher	*Polioptila caerulea*	3,8
Tropical Gnatcatcher	*Polioptila plumbea*	8,12
Veery	*Catharus fuscescens*	12
Gray-cheeked Thrush	*Catharus minimus*	8,12
Swainson's Thrush	*Catharus ustulatus*	8,12
Wood Thrush	*Hylocichla mustelina*	8,12
Clay-colored Robin	*Turdus grayi*	8,9,12
White-throated Robin	*Turdus assimilis*	3,8,12
Gray Catbird	*Dumetella carolinensis*	3,8,12
Black Catbird	*Melanoptila glabrirostris*	8,9
Cedar Waxwing	*Bombycilla cedrorum*	3
White-eyed Vireo	*Vireo griseus*	8,12
Mangrove Vireo	*Vireo pallens*	2,8,9,12
Philadelphia Vireo	*Vireo philadelphicus*	12
Red-eyed Vireo	*Vireo olivaceus*	8,12
Yellow-green Vireo	*Vireo flavoviridis*	8,9,12
Tawny-crowned Greenlet	*Hylophilus ochraceiceps*	8,12
Lesser Greenlet	*Hylophilus decurtatus*	8,12
Green Shrike-Vireo	*Vireolanius pulchellus*	8,12
Blue-winged Warbler	*Vermivora pinus*	12

Common Name	Scientific Name	Records
Tennessee Warbler	*Vermivora peregrina*	12
Yellow Warbler	*Dendroica petechia*	8,12
Chestnut-sided Warbler	*Dendroica pensylvanica*	12
Magnolia Warbler	*Dendroica magnolia*	8,12
Yellow-rumped Warbler (Myrtle)	*Dendroica coronata*	12
Black-throated Green Warbler	*Dendroica virens*	12
Blackburnian Warbler	*Dendroica fusca*	12
. Cerulean Warbler	*Dendroica cerulea*	12
Black-and-white Warbler	*Mniotilta varia*	8,12
American Redstart	*Setophaga ruticilla*	8,12
Prothonotary Warbler	*Protonotaria citrea*	12
Worm-eating Warbler	*Helmitheros vermivorus*	12
Ovenbird	*Seiurus aurocapillus*	8,12
Northern Waterthrush	*Seiurus noveboracensis*	8,12
Louisiana Waterthrush	*Seiurus motacilla*	8,12
Kentucky Warbler	*Oporornis formosus*	8,12
. Mourning Warbler	*Oporornis philadelphia*	8,12
Common Yellowthroat	*Geothlypis trichas*	8,12
Gray-crowned Yellowthroat	*Geothlypis poliocephala*	8
Hooded Warbler	*Wilsonia citrina*	8,12
Wilson's Warbler	*Wilsonia pusilla*	12

Golden-crowned Warbler	*Basileuterus culicivorus*	3,8,12
Yellow-breasted Chat	*Icteria virens*	8,12
Gray-throated Chat	*Granatellus sallaei*	12
Bananaquit	*Coereba flaveola*	8,12
Golden-masked Tanager	*Tangara larvata*	8,12
Green Honeycreeper	*Chlorophanes spiza*	12
Red-legged Honeycreeper	*Cyanerpes cyaneus*	8,12
Scrub Euphonia	*Euphonia affinis*	8
Yellow-throated Euphonia	*Euphonia hirundinacea*	3,8,12
Olive-backed Euphonia	*Euphonia gouldi*	8,12
Blue-gray Tanager	*Thraupis episcopus*	1,3,8
Yellow-winged Tanager	*Thraupis abbas*	1,3,8,9,12
Gray-headed Tanager	*Eucometis penicillata*	8,12
Black-throated Shrike-Tanager	*Lanio aurantius*	8,12
Red-crowned Ant-Tanager	*Habia rubica*	8,12
Red-throated Ant-Tanager	*Habia fuscicauda*	8,9,12
Rose-throated Tanager	*Piranga roseogularis*	8,12
Hepatic Tanager	*Piranga flava*	3 ?
Summer Tanager	*Piranga rubra*	12
.. Flame-colored Tanager	*Piranga bidentata*	8
White-winged Tanager	*Piranga leucoptera*	12

Crimson-collared Tanager	*Ramphocelus sanguinolentus*	1,3
Grayish Saltator	*Saltator coerulescens*	8,9
Black-headed Saltator	*Saltator atriceps*	8,9,11,12
Black-faced Grosbeak	*Caryothraustes poliogaster*	8,12
Northern Cardinal	*Cardinalis cardinalis*	9,12
Rose-breasted Grosbeak	*Pheucticus ludovicianus*	12
Blue-black Grosbeak	*Cyanocompsa cyanoides*	8,12
Blue Bunting	*Cyanocompsa parellina*	8
Blue Grosbeak	*Guiraca caerulea*	8,12
Indigo Bunting	*Passerina cyanea*	8,9,12
Painted Bunting	*Passerina ciris*	1,3,8,9,12
Dickcissel	*Spiza americana*	8,12
Orange-billed Sparrow	*Arremon aurantiirostris*	8,12
Olive Sparrow	*Arremonops rufivirgatus*	12
Green-backed Sparrow	*Arremonops chloronotus*	8,9,12
Blue-black Grassquit	*Volatinia jacarina*	8,9,12
White-collared Seedeater	*Sporophila torqueola*	3,8,9,12
Thick-billed Seed-Finch	*Oryzoborus funereus*	8,12
Yellow-faced Grassquit	*Tiaris olivacea*	2,3,7,8
Botteri's Sparrow	*Aimophila botterii*	2,8
@ Rusty Sparrow	*Aimophila rufescens*	3

Common Name	Scientific Name	Refs
@ Chipping Sparrow	*Spizella passerina*	2,8
.. Grasshopper Sparrow	*Ammodramus savannarum*	2,3,8
. Bobolink	*Dolichonyx oryzivorus*	12
Red-winged Blackbird	*Agelaius phoeniceus*	1,3,8,9
Eastern Meadowlark	*Sturnella magna*	4,8
Melodious Blackbird	*Dives dives*	8,9,12
Great-tailed Grackle	*Quiscalus mexicanus*	8,11
Bronzed Cowbird	*Molothrus aeneus*	8
Giant Cowbird	*Scaphidura oryzivora*	8,11,12
Black-cowled Oriole	*Icterus dominicensis*	8,9,12
Orchard Oriole	*Icterus spurius*	8,11,12
Yellow-tailed Oriole	*Icterus mesomelas*	8,9,11,12
Northern Oriole	*Icterus galbula*	12
Yellow-billed Cacique	*Amblycercus holosericeus*	1,3,9
@ .. Chestnut-headed Oropendola	*Psarocolius wagleri*	11
Montezuma Oropendola	*Psarocolius montezuma*	3,8,11,12

*Reference Footnotes for Specimen Records:

1 = Moore 1859
2 = Salvin 1863 and/or 1866
3 = Salvin and Godman 1879–1904
4 = Sclater 1886
5 = Ogilvie-Grant 1893
6 = Lantz 1899

7 = Ridgway 1901–50
8 = Van Tyne 1935
9 = Taibel 1955
10 = Smithe and Land 1960
11 = Milwaukee Public Museum (unpubl. specimen records)

12 = Smithe and Paynter 1963 and/or Smithe 1966
13 = Land 1970
14 = Traylor 1979
15 = Ellis and Whaley 1981
? = Questionable specimen

Appendix 3: List of Petén Species Based on Sight Record(s) Only

(No specimen records known from Petén – does not include hypotheticals)

(P) Photographed   (S) Sound Recording

Brown Pelican	*Pelecanus occidentalis*
Pinnated Bittern	*Botaurus pinnatus*
.. American Bittern	*Botaurus lentiginosus*
Least Bittern	*Ixobrychus exilis*
Great Blue Heron	*Ardea herodias*
Snowy Egret	*Egretta thula*
Tricolored Heron	*Egretta tricolor*
. Reddish Egret	*Egretta rufescens*
White Ibis	*Eudocimus albus*
Jabiru	*Jabiru mycteria*
Wood Stork	*Mycteria americana*
@ Black-bellied Whistling-Duck	*Dendrocygna autumnalis*
Blue-winged Teal	*Anas dicors*
Northern Shoveler	*Anas clypeata*
.. Ring-necked Duck	*Aythya collaris*
Black Vulture	*Coragyps atratus*
Turkey Vulture	*Cathartes aura*
Lesser Yellow-headed Vulture	*Cathartes burrovianus*
Osprey	*Pandion haliaetus*
Gray-headed Kite	*Leptodon cayanensis*
Black-shouldered Kite	*Elanus caeruleus*
Sharp-shinned Hawk	*Accipiter striatus*
Common Black-Hawk	*Buteogallus anthracinus*

Short-tailed Hawk	*Buteo brachyurus*
Zone-tailed Hawk	*Buteo albonotatus*
Black-and-white Hawk-Eagle (S)	*Spizastur melanoleucus*
Sora	*Porzana carolina*
Common Moorhen (P)	*Gallinula chloropus*
@ Collared Plover	*Charadrius collaris*
Snowy Plover	*Charadrius alexandrinus*
American Avocet	*Recurvirostra americana*
Greater Yellowlegs	*Tringa melanoleuca*
Western Sandpiper	*Calidris mauri*
Least Sandpiper	*Calidris minutilla*
Stilt Sandpiper	*Calidris himantopus*
Common Snipe	*Gallinago gallinago*
Wilson's Phalarope	*Phalaropus tricolor*
Laughing Gull	*Larus atricilla*
Ring-billed Gull	*Larus delawarensis*
Royal Tern	*Sterna maxima*
Rock Dove	*Columba livia*
Red-billed Pigeon	*Columba flavirostris*
Mourning Dove	*Zenaida macroura*
Black-billed Cuckoo	*Coccyzus erythropthalmus*
Yellow-billed Cuckoo	*Coccyzus americanus*
Striped Cuckoo	*Tapera naevia*
Ferruginous Pygmy-Owl (P)	*Glaucidium brasilianum*
Lesser Nighthawk	*Chordeiles acutipennis*
Common Nighthawk	*Chordeiles minor*
White-collared Swift	*Streptoprocne zonaris*
Chimney Swift	*Chaetura pelagica*
Lesser Swallow-tailed Swift (P)	*Panyptila cayennensis*
Black-crested Coquette (P)	*Lophornis helenae*
. Keel-billed Motmot	*Electron carinatum*
Rufous-breasted Spinetail (S)	*Synallaxis erythrothorax*
Greater Pewee	*Contopus pertinax*

@.. Black Phoebe *Sayornis nigricans*
Lovely Cotinga (P) *Cotinga amabilis*
Purple Martin *Progne subis*
Tree Swallow *Tachycineta bicolor*
Bank Swallow *Riparia riparia*
Cliff Swallow *Hirundo pyrrhonota*
Tropical Mockingbird *Mimus gilvus*
Solitary Vireo *Vireo solitarius*
Yellow-throated Vireo *Vireo flavifrons*
Warbling Vireo *Vireo gilvus*
Rufous-browed Peppershrike *Cyclarhis gujanensis*
Golden-winged Warbler *Vermivora chrysoptera*
Orange-crowned Warbler *Vermivora celata*
Nashville Warbler *Vermivora ruficapilla*
Northern Parula *Parula americana*
Tropical Parula *Parula pitiayumi*
Cape May Warbler *Dendroica tigrina*
Yellow-throated Warbler *Dendroica dominica*
Bay-breasted Warbler *Dendroica castanea*
Swainson's Warbler *Limnothlypis swainsonii*
Canada Warbler *Wilsonia canadensis*
Scarlet Tanager *Piranga olivacea*
.. Western Tanager *Piranga ludoviciana*
@ Scarlet-rumped Tanager *Ramphocelus passerinii*
Buff-throated Saltator *Saltator maximus*
Yellow-backed Oriole *Icterus chrysater*
Altamira Oriole *Icterus gularis*

Observation Notes

Species:

Date:

Specific locality:

Habitat description:

Field marks of bird:

Behavioral description (perched, foraging/flight patterns, canopy height, song/call, etc.):

Optics used:

Observer(s) name(s):

Observer(s) familiarity with species:

Check any other documentation obtained, if applicable:

☐ Photograph   ☐ Sound recording   ☐ Sketch

Please return to: Randy Beavers, Science Center,
8856 Westview Drive, Houston, TX 77055 USA

Selected References
*- recommended for field use in Tikal.

American Ornithologists' Union. 1983. *Check-list of North American birds.* 6th ed. Washington, D.C.: American Ornithologists' Union.

———. 1985. Thirty-fifth supplement to the American Ornithologists' Union *Check-list of North American birds. Auk* 102:680–86.

———. 1987. Thirty-sixth supplement to the American Ornithologists' Union *Check-list of North American birds. Auk* 104:591–96.

———. 1989. Thirty-seventh supplement to the American Ornithologists' Union *Check-list of North American birds. Auk* 106:532–38.

———. 1991. Thirty-eighth supplement to the American Ornithologists' Union *Check-list of North American birds. Auk* 108:750–54.

Beavers, R. A., D. J. Delaney, C. W. Leahy, and G. F. Oatman. 1991. New and noteworthy bird records from Petén, Guatemala, including Tikal National Park. *Bull. Brit. Ornith. Club* 111:77–90.

Binford, L. C. 1989. *A distributional survey of the birds of the Mexican state of Oaxaca.* Ornithological Monograph No. 43. Washington, D.C.: American Ornithologists' Union.

Blake, E. R. 1953. *Birds of Mexico: A guide for field identification.* Chicago: Univ. of Chicago Press.

————. 1977. *Manual of neotropical birds.* Vol. 1. Chicago: Univ. of Chicago Press.

Box, B. 1990. *1990 South American handbook.* 66th ed. New York: Prentice Hall Trade.

Brodkin, H., and P. Brodkin. 1981. Summer birds at Polol, Guatemala. *Continental Birdlife* 2:111–17.

Burnham, W. A., J. P. Jenny, and C. W. Turley. 1988, 1989, 1990. *Progress reports I, II, and III. Maya project: Investigation of raptors and their habitats as environmental indicators for preserving biodiversity and tropical forests of Latin America.* Boise, Idaho: Peregrine Fund, Inc. World Center for Birds of Prey.

Carr, R. F., and J. E. Hazard. 1961. *Map of the ruins of Tikal, El Petén, Guatemala.* Univ. Mus. Tikal Report No. 11. Philadelphia: Univ. of Pennsylvania.

Coe, W. R. 1967. *Tikal: A handbook of the ancient Maya ruins.* Philadelphia: Univ. Mus. Univ. of Pennsylvania.

Davis, L. I. 1972. *A field guide to the birds of Mexico and Central America.* Austin: Univ. of Texas Press.

Dickerman, R. W. 1975. Nine new specimen records for Guatemala. *Wilson Bull.* 87: 412–13.

Edwards, E. P. 1959. Nesting of Lesser Swallow-tailed Swift in Guatemala. *Auk* 76:358–59.

————. 1989. *A field guide to the birds of Mexico.* Sweet Briar, Va.: E. P. Edwards.

Eisenmann, E. 1955. *The species of Middle American birds.* Trans. Linnaean Soc. New York. Vol. 7. New York.

————. 1971. Range expansion and population increase in

North and Middle America of the White-tailed Kite (*Elanus leucurus*). *Amer. Birds* 25:529–36.

Ellis, D. H., and W. H. Whaley. 1981. Three Crested Eagle records for Guatemala. *Wilson Bull.* 93:284–85.

Griscom, L. 1932. *The distribution of bird-life in Guatemala.* American Mus. Nat. Hist. Bull. 64. New York.

Hellmayr, C. E. (and B. Conover, pt. 1; and C. B. Cory, pts. 2–3). 1924–49. *Catalogue of birds of the Americas.* Field Mus. Nat. Hist. Zool. Series Vol. 13 (11 pts.). Chicago.

Holdridge, L. R. 1967. *Life zone ecology.* San Jose, Costa Rica: Tropical Science Center.

Howell, S. N. G. 1989. Mexico, Belize – Regional summary of the 89th (1988) Christmas bird count. *Amer. Birds* 43: 1210–11.

Isler, M. L., and P. R. Isler. 1987. *The tanagers.* Washington, D.C.: Smithsonian Institution Press.

* Land, H. C. 1970. *Birds of Guatemala.* Wynnewood, Pa.: Livingston Publishing.

Land, H.C., and W. L. Schultz. 1963. A proposed subspecies of the Great Potoo, *Nyctibius grandis* (Gmelin). *Auk* 80: 195–96.

Lantz, D. E. 1899. A list of birds collected by Col. N. S. Goss in Mexico and Central America. *Trans. Kansas Acad. Sci.* 16:218–24.

Lundell, C. L., 1937. *The vegetation of Petén.* Carnegie Inst. of Wash. Publ. 478. Washington, D.C.

———. 1961. The flora of Tikal. *Expedition* 3:38–43.

Lynch, J. F. 1989. Distribution of overwintering Nearctic migrants in the Yucatán Peninsula. I: General patterns of occurrence. *Condor* 91:515–44.

Mason, C. R. 1976. Cape May Warblers in middle America. *Auk* 93:167–69.

Monroe, B. L., Jr. 1968. *A distributional survey of the birds of Honduras.* Ornithological Monograph No. 7. Washington, D.C.: American Ornithologists' Union.

Moore, T. J. 1859. List of mammals and birds collected by Joseph Leyland in Honduras, Belize, and Guatemala. *Proc. Zool. Soc. of London* 1859:50–65.

* National Geographic Society. 1987. *Field guide to the birds of North America.* 2d ed. Washington, D.C.: National Geographic Soc.

Ogilvie-Grant, W. R. 1893. *Catalogue of the birds of the British Museum.* Vol. 22. London: Trustees of the British Mus.

Page, J. L. 1938. The climate of Petén, Guatemala. In *The inscriptions of Petén,* by S. G. Morley. Washington, D.C.: Carnegie Inst. of Wash. Publ. 437(IV): 349–53.

Paynter, R. A., Jr. 1955. *The ornithogeography of the Yucatán Peninsula.* Peabody Mus. Nat. Hist. Bull. 9. New Haven: Yale Univ.

Peters, J. L., et al. 1933–87. *Check-list of birds of the world.* 16 vols. Mus. Comp. Zool. Harvard Univ. Cambridge.

Peterson, R. T. 1963. *A field guide to the birds of Texas.* Boston: Houghton Mifflin.

———. 1980. *A field guide to birds of eastern and central North America.* Boston: Houghton Mifflin.

———. 1990. *A field guide to western birds.* Boston: Houghton Mifflin.

* Peterson, R. T., and E. L. Chalif. 1973. *A field guide to Mexican birds.* Boston: Houghton Mifflin.

Phillips, A. R. 1986–91. *The known birds of North and Middle America.* 2 pts. Denver: Allan R. Phillips.

Rangel-Salazar, J. L., and J. H. Vega-Rivera. 1989. Two new records of birds for southern Mexico. *Condor* 91:214–15.

Ridgway, R. (and H. Friedmann, pts. 9–11). 1901–50. *The birds of North and Middle America*. U.S. Natl. Mus. Bull. 50 (11 pts.). Washington, D.C.

Robbins, C. S., B. Bruun, and H. S. Zim. 1983. *Birds of North America: A guide to field identification*. New York: Golden Press.

Russell, S. M. 1964. *A distributional study of the birds of British Honduras*. Ornithological Monograph No. 1. Washington, D.C.: American Ornithologists' Union.

Salvin, O. 1863. Description of thirteen new species of birds discovered in Central America by F. D. Godman and O. Salvin. *Proc. Zool. Soc. of London* 1863:186–90.

———. 1866. A further contribution to the ornithology of Guatemala. *Ibis* 1866:188–206.

Salvin, O., and F. D. Godman. 1879–1904. *Biologia Centrali Americana: Aves*. 3 vols. London: Taylor and Francis.

Saunders, G. B., A. D. Holloway, and C. O. Handley, Jr. 1950. The game birds and shorebirds of Guatemala. *U.S. Dept. Int. Fish and Wildlife Serv. Spec. Sci. Report* 5:3–98.

Sclater, P. L. 1886. *Catalogue of the birds of the British Museum*. Vol. 11. London: Trustees of the British Mus.

Sclater, P. L., and O. Salvin. 1859. Contributions to the ornithology of Central America. *Ibis* 1859:1–22, 117–38, 213–34.

Skutch, A. F. 1954. *Life histories of Central American birds*. Vol. 1. Pacific Coast Avifauna Series No. 31. Berkeley, Calif.: Cooper Ornith. Soc.

———. 1960. *Life histories of Central American birds*. Vol. 2.

Pacific Coast Avifauna Series No. 34. Berkeley, Calif.: Cooper Ornith. Soc.

————. 1967. *Life histories of Central American birds.* Vol. 3. Pacific Coast Avifauna Series No. 35. Berkeley, Calif.: Cooper Ornith. Soc.

————. 1972. *Studies of tropical American birds.* Nuttall Ornith. Club Publ. 10. Cambridge, Mass.

————. 1981. *New studies of tropical American birds.* Nuttall Ornith. Club Publ. 19. Cambridge, Mass.

* Smithe, F. B. 1966. *The birds of Tikal.* Garden City, N.J.: Natural History Press.

Smithe, F. B., and H. C. Land. 1960. First record of Cattle Egrets in Guatemala. *Auk* 77:218.

Smithe, F. B., and R. A. Paynter, Jr. 1963. Birds of Tikal, Guatemala. *Bull. Harvard Univ. Mus. Comp. Zool.* 128: 245–324.

Solis, P., J. Vankirk, P. Vankirk and P. L. Vankirk. 1976. *Tikal, Guatemala.* Guatemala City, Guatemala: Filmtrek.

Taibel, A. M. 1955. Uccelli del Guatemala con speciale riguardo alla region del Petén raccolti dal Maggio al Settembre 1932. *Atti Societa Italiana di Scienze Naturali* 94:15–84.

Traylor, M. A., Jr. 1979. Two sibling species of *Tyrannus* (Tyrannidae). *Auk* 96:221–23.

Van Tyne, J. 1935. *The birds of Northern Petén, Guatemala.* Univ. Mich. Mus. Zool. Misc. Publ. 27. Ann Arbor.

Wadell, H. 1938. Physical-geological features of Petén, Guatemala. In *The inscriptions of Petén,* by S. G. Morley. Carnegie Inst. of Wash. Publ. 437(IV): 336–48.

Wendelken, P. W., and R. F. Martin. 1986. Recent data on the distribution of birds in Guatemala. *Bull. Brit. Ornith. Club* 106:16–21.

Wood, D. S., R. C. Leberman, and D. Weyer. 1986. *Checklist of the birds of Belize.* Spec. Publ. No. 12. Pittsburgh: Carnegie Mus. Nat. Hist.

Index to Families, Genera, and Common Names

152   INDEX

Notes